Contemporary

Pottery Decoration

*To my dearest wife Judy, whose support
and understanding makes all things possible.*

Contemporary
Pottery Decoration

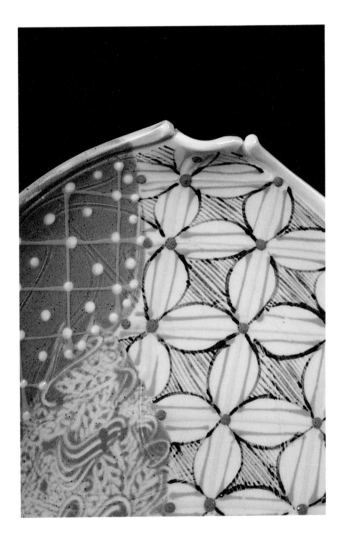

· JOHN GIBSON ·

Chilton Book Company
Radnor, Pennsylvania

Published in Radnor, Pennsylvania 19089.
by Chilton Book Company
First published 1987 by A & C Black (Publishers) Ltd
35 Bedford Row, London WC1R 4JH

Library of Congress Catalog Card 87-4729

ISBN 0-8019-7808-4

Jacket illustrations
front: detail from plate by John Gibson
(photo by John Coles)
back: detail from dish by Archie McCall
(photo by Jonathan Robertson)

Photograph on Contents page is a detail
of work by Daphne Carnegy

Filmset in 11/13 Palatino by August Filmsetting, Haydock.
Printed in Hong Kong by South China Printing Company.

Contents

Acknowledgements

I take this opportunity to extend my deep-felt thanks to all of the potters who have given so much of their time and help to enable this book to happen. I send particular thanks to overseas potters whose prompt and enthusiastic response has widened the scope of the book. Special thanks to John Coles whose photography of the British potters not only superbly illustrates the techniques and products, but are sensitive studies in themselves. Thank you to Jonathan Robertson for photographing the work of Archie McCall. Thanks to Judith Holden, my editor. Finally my best regards to Ray Ashcroft for beer and sympathy and Peter Stewart for plying me with champagne and supplying the typewriter.

Introduction

As a maker myself, I am passionately concerned with pottery decoration, so when first asked to write a book on the subject I naturally wanted to give as full a view of it as possible. But I soon realised that to do the subject full justice I would have to extend this book to many volumes, describing the history and development of ceramics worldwide. I began to rethink what I might cover, and decided to look at contemporary approaches to decoration, focusing on the ideas and techniques of a small representative group of today's makers. Yet because of the time-lag between compiling information and publishing a book any work illustrated can only indicate one stage in the development of a potter's progress, and this book can therefore only freeze moments in the constantly changing world of pottery making.

Although I have concentrated upon modern decorated pottery, that subject is too diverse to allow me to catalogue the whole range of clay objects now being produced, so some further decisions had to be made – how was I to choose from the exciting and extensive range of decorated studio ceramics available? Who was to be included and more important, who would be excluded? The final choice of the sixteen potters featured here reflects my own natural predisposition towards vessels and vessel makers. I hope to give readers a deeper understanding of each potter's motivations and work. I have tried to cover fully each featured potter's work, from the conception of an idea to the finished pot, discussing philosophy, inspiration, techniques and choice of motif, not presenting a dry step-by-step manual of decoration techniques but trying to illustrate the reasons why as well as how we decorate our work. Skills and techniques can be learned and understood, yet how we use those skills and what influences us in our decisions is not just interesting in itself but important to the quality of a finished piece.

Each of the stages from forming to firing has a bearing on the finished pot, so I decided to look at work within the framework of the temperature to which it is subjected when fired. Chapter 1 deals with potters who work within low temperature ranges; chapter 2 with earthenware and the mid ranges; chapter 3 with stoneware and porcelain; chapter 4 features makers of salt glaze stoneware, and chapter 5 deals with post-firing decoration such as onglaze enamels and lustres. I have also included in each chapter a selection of illustrations showing work by other potters who are firing within these temperature ranges. Although most of the pieces illustrated fit within such temperature boundaries, there are some potters whose work lies upon the 'cusp' and others whose main body of work lies within one temperature but may be finished in another, perhaps with the addition of small amounts of lustres or onglaze enamels.

Certain attitudes emerged from the mass of ideas and information collected, threading through much of the work I saw, albeit with variation. The makers all have an intense commitment to the quality and finish of their work, and without exception know intimately the limitations of the tools and materials they employ, yet they constantly extend their use of these tools and materials to discover new ways of working. All sixteen potters are true to the physical and emotional influences which act upon them, and translating those influences into personal forms, colours and motifs is a strong part of their work.

The recent advances made in the quality and supply of raw materials, such as underglaze colours and stains, the progress being made in kiln design and insulation, and the amount of technical information published have all contributed to an exciting period in ceramics. A very wide colour range is now available in all firing ranges and with all methods of colour application; kilns are now more portable, cleaner and less bulky, allowing for more compact studios. The circulation of illustrated ceramic books and journals is breaking down international barriers, and bringing work from many cultures to our attention. These developments offer an increasing freedom of expression to potters – imagination is no longer bound by technical restrictions or by unavailable materials, and this has, to some extent, led to more experimental attitudes to decoration, as opposed to a particular adherence to formula and recipe. Many of the potters I talked to were using colour in a very painterly way, mixing their palettes by eye and rule of thumb rather than by percentage weight or molecular formula. With this new freedom have come creative methods of colour application, spraying, stamping, painting and smearing to name but a few, as well as more traditional methods such as slip trailing. All the featured vessel makers mention a variety of significant influences on their work, which range from the thoughts and writings of Matisse, the rugged British coastal waters to a riot of fruit and flowers found growing in some Mediterranean garden. But whatever our influences may be, we now seem to have a larger capacity to translate them into three-dimensional objects.

I do not see this book as making a definitive statement about the nature of contemporary ceramic decoration, but as an illumination of the ideas and techniques of a few modern vessel makers; I hope that it will encourage the reader to investigate further the rich and multi-faceted world of contemporary ceramics. I have tried to offer an insight into some of the reasons why and how a small group of potters decorate their work. Why we should want to decorate anything at all I leave for the reader to decide and for more learned people than myself to write about. My own belief is that we are whatever we make and that our innermost fears, aspirations, hopes and visions are all laid bare when we offer our work to the public. I hope this book will contribute to a greater understanding of an aspect of ceramics with which I myself am deeply involved – and I hope, too, that the book will be read with the same sensitivity as a maker brings to the creation of a pot.

John Maltby (UK)
'Flowers and a Cloud', covered pot 8 inches × 6 inches. Stoneware, glaze resist with red and blue enamels.

Dorothy Feibleman (USA)
Hand-built vessel, inlaid and laminated.

· 1 ·

Low temperature decoration

Featured in this first chapter are potters who fire their work within a low temperature range, somewhere between 600°C to 1000°C. Traditionally, low temperature fired work is created in low technology cultures; little equipment other than clay and combustible material is needed to produce functional vessels. Yet even the most primitive examples of early pottery vessels show some attempt to produce patterns, marks and images upon the pot's surface which relate to religious or social influences – or perhaps they may simply be a joyous expression of the potter's pleasure in creating the vessel.

Technological advances have to some extent broadened the horizons of today's low firing studio vessel makers, who are no longer limited to the use of a local clay, or to firing with easily available material.

Potters may differ widely in approach, yet all the pieces shown in this chapter share qualities in common which occur whenever clay is subjected to a low temperature firing. The vessel will be porous unless a low melting glaze is used, but this glaze will be soft in its fluid adhesion to the pot, and the interface between clay and glaze will be markedly defined. The surface of the pot may to some extent be sealed by applying and burnishing a small-particled slip and this will give a polished silky feel to the surface. Because the pots are porous, carbon particles can be trapped in the surface when they are smoked in combustible materials like sawdust, and this process can be exploited for its decorative qualities. Previous low technology cultures gained this fire patterning on their pottery as a by-product of the firing process, but increasingly con-

temporary makers are using smoked and fire-flashed surfaces for their expressive qualities, recognising the strong emotions that the physical activity of living fire can evoke in us all.

In some of the work of Judy Trim we see the marks made by smoke and flame after her pots have been covered and fired in gently smouldering sawdust, creating a rich and random smoke pattern on the surface of clay, slips and lustres. Fiona Salazar's search for the pared down and unfettered object is supported by her interest in low firing methods – her simple vessel forming techniques and warm burnished surfaces are comparatively direct and uncluttered, apparently far from technical innovation and gimmicks. On the other hand, technical advances have enabled Susan and Steven Kemenyffy to break free from restrictions in scale and concept which have been associated with traditional types of raku firings. In the raku process pots are drawn from the kiln whilst the glaze is flowing and still molten and then subjected to a rapid cooling in combustible material, often in water too; historically, raku pots have been on a small scale, such as the tea bowls and other vessels used in the Japanese tea ceremony. The Kemenyffy's large scale collaborative work is made possible by a hard-won understanding of their materials and how the processes can be worked.

Other work illustrated in this chapter gives an idea of the possibilities open to potters firing within low temperature ranges. The clarity of line of David Roberts' coil-built raku bottles is enhanced by the fine network of crackle lines in the glaze. David Miller's free drawing complements the soft plastic modelling of his forms. He uses low temperature coloured slips, glazes and stains and then fires to 980 – 1000°C in a salt vapour. Bennett Bean's work illustrates the possibilities of using colours other than those derived from ceramic materials – he uses acrylic paint to highlight certain masked-out areas produced during the making and firing process.

Bennett Bean (USA)
White earthenware, thrown, burnished and covered in thick terra sigillata before polishing. After biscuit firing areas are resisted with cut tape and wax, salt is sprinkled on the wet wax to create a speckled effect. The piece is then glazed with a thin wash. The piece is placed in a topless concrete box (to protect from heat shock) covered in wood and fired. The exposed resisted areas are painted with acrylic paint and the piece is sealed with urethane gel.

Judy Trim

'All my forms are vessels; the intrinsic act of containing never ceases to intrigue me, with its endless actual and symbolic possibilities. For me the pot has a strong analogy with the feminine principle; its function is to hold, to preserve, to protect, to receive and to give out. The pot is centred about its cavity and my time is spent struggling towards finding a way of conveying mystery, potency and sensuality, through the building of the inner space, in the hope that the accumulation of sensations from these hand-made, unrepeatable forms contain a relevance to here and now and reflect some measure of still essence.'

The strong beliefs which support Judy Trim's work are rooted in her training as a painter and potter at the Bath Academy of Art, Corsham, Wiltshire. At this college she found the initial impetus to work with ceramics from her tutors John Colbeck and James Tower. Then she taught painting and pottery full-time to children in central London schools, until personal circumstances allowed her the freedom to concentrate solely on her own pottery ideas and techniques, working in the studio at the rear of her home in north London. This proved to be a time of experiment and play—Judy worked totally by herself for three years, re-discovering materials and exploring the effects of sawdust firings. Certain contemporary potters were influential with regard to philosophy, form and decorative technique; the work of Hans Coper, Lucie Rie and Elizabeth Fritsch was important to many of Judy's early forms, which were also influenced by Egyptian, American-Indian and Cycladic forms.

'The way I feel about the influence of others is reflected in the words of Matisse, who said "I have never avoided the influence of others; I would have considered this a cowardice and a lack of sincerity towards myself. I believe the personality of the artist develops and asserts itself through the struggles it has to go through when pitted against other personalities. If the fight is fatal and the personality succumbs it means this was bound to be its fate." '*

Continually looking, drawing, extracting and building upon shapes derived from nature (an approach encouraged at Bath Academy) Judy's forms reflect her interest in seed pods, fossils, shells and so on. All her pots are coiled, a process which for her is very slow and painstaking but extremely enjoyable because of the absolute control which is possible. She began by making simple, round shapes but then introduced oval, square and oblong shapes.

Judy's forms remain within a fairly simple range, yet she is constantly developing the shapes, pushing, extending, and stretching the forms in subtle ways, using each nuance and variation which emerges during a pot's construction as the basis for the next piece to be made. All Judy's pots are footless—she is fascinated by pots which balance on the

*the quotations from Matisse are taken from *Matisse on Art* by Jack D. Flam (Phaidon 1978)

smallest possible base, by the danger and excitement such forms offer and the quality of airiness which they may possess. And she pushes the boundaries to an extreme, her almost fatal fascination with the impossibility of form indicating a nature which wants to reach to the limits but retain full control over the point at which to stop.

Judy sees herself primarily as a form builder, but she has always had a strong desire to decorate her environment, and this has been progressively reflected in her work. She first started using sawdust firings when working with children in schools, and she became very interested in the powerful, primitive qualities of fire, 'smoking' her pots by placing them in smouldering sawdust. Using the sensuous textures and subtle palette of colours offered by this firing method absorbed her for many years.

Gradually her work evolved and she started to decorate some of her pieces with simple geometric designs, using coloured slips and oxides – then later the coloured slips were burnished and later still she began to add lustres to the burnished surfaces. However, some of her work remains concerned purely with form, and these pots are often simply burnished and smoked. Most recently her work has been conceived and constructed along four separate themes, although all four have strong links with each other; Judy always maintains a body of work around her to feed on whilst making each new piece.

The first of these four categories are white pots, using T. material for strength and texture. These pots are usually made in groups of twos and threes. These tall, elegant, narrow-based flasks are cool, soaring columns, large in scale and concept – pure, powerful and simple. Their beginnings are found in Judy's response to long thin shells and column forms, and the pots have surfaces which show many shades of white.

Judy's second group of pots are beaker forms and are on a more intimate scale. She uses red clay, sometimes burnished with slips, smoking the pots to show an earthy, black, red and white surface in many combinations, creating warm, mysteriously sensual effects.

Her third group of pots are tear jars, which have strong reference to Roman and Egyptian glass tear jars. Finally she makes flaring, large, open dishes which start from the smallest possible base and extend to soaring, wide, open rims. These pots are generous in expression, celebratory, glittering and flamboyant.

'A quotation by Matisse sums up more succinctly than I could my philosophical concern with the matter of making objects: "It seems to me that the way art may be said to imitate nature is by the life that the creative worker infuses into that work of art; the work will then appear as fertile and as possessed of the same power to thrill, the same

2 A coloured lustre is painted onto the central motif.

1 Many of Judy's ideas for decorative motifs and colour combinations are carried through on tiles. A slipped and burnished fired tile has a design etched into the surface using a nail and steel rule.

3 A contrasting lustre is painted around the border.

resplendent beauty that we find in the works of nature. Great love is needed to achieve this effect, a love capable of inspiring and sustaining, that patient striving towards truth, that flowing warmth and an analytic profundity that accompanies the birth of any work of art; but is not love the origin of all creation?"'

4 A simple sawdust kiln is constructed in the garden.

Simplicity is the key word in Judy's approach to ceramic technique and technology. She uses just two clays, T. material and a red earthenware. T. material has good drying strength, with an open, coarse texture, fires white and is suitable for the forms which are large or precipitous in shape. Red earthenware is warm and earthy in texture and colour and it will take the smoke well in sawdust firings.

Each coiled piece begins with a very small piece of clay which forms the base, on which thin coils of clay are added and refined by scraping the form, which is frequently inverted (until too large to accommodate this method) over the stem of a hat stand. She uses only one basic white slip, consisting of 50% china clay and 50% white ball clay. All of the colouring agents added to the slip, whether commercial stain or metal oxide, are added by eye, and here Judy's experience and training as a painter comes into play. If a large piece is to be burnished, then the slip is painted on whilst the pot is under construction; coloured slips are sprayed on to surfaces which won't be burnished. When biscuit fired (between 900°C and 1000°C) the surface of the fired-on coloured slip is often scratched with a sharp tool. Areas of the biscuit fired pots are often painted with lustres, building up layers of rich vibrant colours after multiple firings at around 750°C.

Judy keeps references in the form of many decorated test tiles. Much of her decoration consists of simple geometrical patterns and colour plays an important role in her work; her tall white pots have subtle surface colours, blue-white, pink-white and yellow-white. Her large open dishes are bright, using hot reds, oranges, golds and blue to evoke images of the summer sun, whereas a winter sun dish uses paler colours, cool yellows and silvers. She also makes star bowls and moon bowls. Lustres offer her the opportunity of extending her palette; overpainting, inter-mixing and multiple firings provide a wide range of possibilities to explore.

5–6 Several small kilns have been built, some containing finished pots, some containing test pieces. After being ignited at the top the combustible material will burn down slowly.

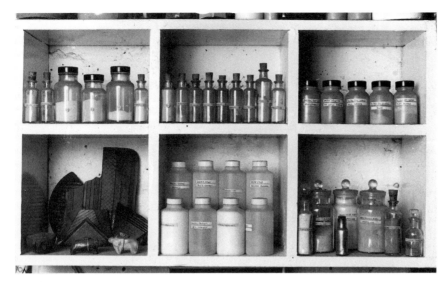

Some of the wide range of enamels, under and overglaze colours, lustres and raw materials used by Judy.

Below: A small selection of test tiles showing a variety of motifs.

'All the things that I make are to do with how I feel, not with how I eat and drink; I have something I want to produce and it is concerned with an emotion, but there is a craft attached to it, perhaps not unlike the sort of skill that was involved in painting, in the days when the artist had to know how to grind and make the colours he used. The kinds of emotions that I am concerned with are summed up by the composer Michael Tippett who said recently "the artist's function in society today is still what it always was, to create from the depths of the imagination and to give them form, images from the past, shapes of the future, images of vigour for a decadent period, images of calm for one too violent, images of hope and reconciliation for worlds torn by division and in an age of mediocracy and shattered dreams, images of abounding, generous, exuberant beauty"'.

Nothing that Judy Trim makes can be seen in isolation from the way in which she perceives her life and the environment she creates for herself. The pots she makes are the physical embodiment of deeply held beliefs; the simple, evocative symbolism of individual and inter-related objects, her instinctive response to form and colour combined with her direct, simple construction methods create works of significant beauty which are an important contribution to contemporary ceramics.

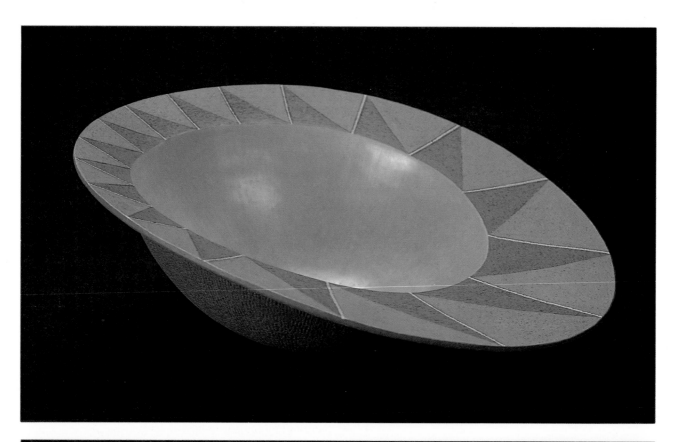

Above: 'Small Sun Bowl', c. 14 inches diameter, 1985. T. material with burnished and painted coloured slips.

Below: 'Large Summer Sun Bowl', c. 25 inches diameter, 1986. T. material with burnished slips and metal lustres.

Photography by John Coles.

16

'Square Flask',
c. 24 inches high,
1984. T. Material
with sprayed slip
and slip inlay.

Susan and Steven Kemenyffy

Susan and Steven Kemenyffy trained in two separate disciplines, printmaking and pottery respectively, both gaining masters degrees from the University of Iowa. They have combined their skills with a knowledge of raku firing and the techniques of making low fired glazed ware to produce pieces of monumental structure with rich colourful surfaces. Steven is responsible primarily for all the three-dimensional manipulation of the clay as well as firing all the biscuit and glaze kilns while Susan has responsibility for drawing and glazing. They first began to work together by experimenting on a single piece, during the waiting time before the birth of their daughter Maya, and the collaboration offers both of them an opportunity to pursue personal aesthetic concerns while still working within the parameters dictated by the exacting nature of raku.

'We are usually careful not to encroach on each other's aesthetic territory, long ago discovering that to work together successfully we must believe in the professionalism and certitude of each other. In the best pieces this system works. The clay possesses an energy and a mystery which is greater than our individual efforts.'

Susan and Steven live on 47 acres of rural land in north-west Pennsylvania, within a few miles of Lake Erie. In this location is a 35 × 70 ft steel horse barn, which acts as a studio; another studio has been built onto this, so that each working area is separate but the whole forms a joint working area, with a solid wall and an opaque door between the two studios.

Steven begins the making process by bringing tons of clay from the mixing room into his studio where he begins to make the forms and objects, mostly wall hangings and freestanding forms. These are eventually transferred to Susan's studio through the connecting door and down a gently sloping ramp. Steven can claim these forms to be his alone; it is his decision to provide fat or thin, tall or squat forms which Susan assesses and whose surface she manipulates prior to marking and painting. No consultations are entered into — there is only the endless process of damp forms waiting for completion by Susan.

'We never discuss our work together in any stage of its creation. I never know what shapes will come through the door between our studios.'

Susan begins the surface decoration by drawing directly onto the leatherhard forms with india ink and a brush — she usually has a life model present in the studio at this stage. The drawings are done freely and swiftly with one overriding emphasis, that being to wed successfully the two-dimensional surface quality with the three-dimensional sculptural aspect of the pieces. Although continually evolving, her subject matter has remained broadly constant since the beginning; her drawings almost always include women and also often show plants and foliage; she also has an elegant collection of hats in her studio which makes its way into the drawings too. She and Steven have planted extensive gardens, and her decoration reflects this interest:

'From the first crocuses to the last frosted chrysanthemums, flower forms provide supplemental subject matter for the 'women who wait' as someone once described the raku ladies. The south studio is so hospitable that from the onslaught of winter to the onset of spring plants thrive in the cool moist whiteness, continuing to flower and bringing new patterns to my drawings.'

18

After the initial drawings are completed in ink and they appear to be spatially appropriate to the contour and texture of the sculptural work then the model leaves and the business of selecting lines and incising the ink with a ceramic needle begins. Selected edges are made permanent by these incisions through the surface of the leatherhard forms. The incising acts in two ways—firstly it delineates the drawing and secondly it restrains the flow and movement of melting glazes during the firing process, maintaining a coherent image. Control of the movement of the glazes and their effect on the ultimate drawing is of paramount importance because of the intense and rapid changes in atmosphere during post-firing; the reduction and oxidation of the surface colours can become so arbitrary at this time that to contribute any more to that arbitrariness in the drawing and glazing process could lead to objects of pure chaos.

After incising the pieces are left to dry for a few days. In summer they are taken to the sun-drenched gardens and in winter they are set beneath overhead radiant heaters which heat the thirty-five hundred square feet of studios. When dry they are taken by Steven back up the ramp and gingerly placed in the biscuit kiln. The unheated west end of the original horse barn contains two kilns: a 100 cu.ft biscuit kiln, and a 16 cu.ft glaze kiln used primarily for wall forms. Clay storing and mixing areas as well as packing and shipping areas are nearby. Two adjacent sheds house a third 20 cu.ft glaze kiln used for sculptures and also a reduction pit.

The pieces are fired in the biscuit kilns from eight to sixteen hours to a temperature of cone 06; they emerge at a final weight of between 20 to 100 lb (15% smaller than when first made). After the biscuit firing the work is unpacked and lightly sanded to removed any burred edges left from having incised the clay. Compressed air is employed to blow away any dust that is left, and then the work is returned to Susan for glazing. At this point the soft monochromatic look of black ink on wet clay has given way to the chalky pinkness of a successful biscuit firing. Barely visible moving patterns of lines recall the burned-out ink drawings, reminding Susan of her original intentions. The glazes are meticulously applied within the etched lines. Some are commercially prepared, for the sake of simplicity, purchased from suppliers in Indiana, Maryland and Colorado; other are mixed at her request to Steven's formulations. Because of the unpredictable nature of the raku process, glazing is considered in terms of contrasting tonal values, dark and light, rather than colour.

Previous page: 'At the Edge of Spring and Water', approximately 42 × 18 × 10 inches, raku sculpture, 1985.

1 Below: Susan working on a design in her studio

2–5 Opposite: Susan and Steven assembling press-moulded clay elements.

'If a 'dubonnet' glaze decides to change from its usual appearance of a red pink to blue glaze it makes little difference but if the scheme were meant to employ a light value colour to bring the form forward and the glaze went dark instead, the structure of the drawing would be unbalanced, thus interfering with the perception of the form as a whole.'

Susan uses a wide palette of colours, from several kinds of white, both translucent and opaque, through almost all the rainbow colours, to many lustrous coppers and blacks. Blue and green glazes are seldom used, perhaps because of the abundance of those colours in the gardens. Allowing herself a choice from the very subtle to the most vibrant of colours offers Susan a broad expressive range.

When Susan is as satisfied as she can be with the application of glazes, the work is returned to Steven for glaze firing. The kilns are fired by natural gas and have a cone activated mechanism which turns them off automatically. Steven constructs them of insulating firebrick, making them highly energy efficient. Cone $5\frac{1}{2}$ is used for glaze firing, which takes approximately $2\frac{1}{2}$ hours, though large sculptures are fired for longer periods. The sculptures may require two or three people to manoeuvre them when plucked from the intense heat to be placed in the waiting pits. The difficulty of getting such large pieces through this type of frenetic process has been somewhat alleviated by the addition of a high percentage of non-plastic kyanite (35 mesh) which helps the work to tolerate the massive thermal shock that it encounters when taken from the red-hot kiln and laid in a cardboard lined trench, to cool in a fluctuating, writhing atmosphere of reduction and oxidation. The pieces remain in the pit for about an hour until they are slightly cooler than the 1800° they reached in the kiln.

'On those days when the kilns are completing the cycle of work the tension is palpable, because it is now that those invested energies and skills, in partnership with the independent contribution of the kiln, bring forth objects of unknown quality; it is that minute between the removal of the kiln door and the frantic placement of the piece in the wide shallow trench lined with cardboard that ultimately determines the fineness of the piece.'

Although their work is based on traditional raku methods, Susan and Steven have evolved their own approach to raku working:

'Raku as we have come to employ the process is an amalgam of three cultures and their ceramic techniques, the Japanese, the south-western American-Indian and the Persian. To the traditional act of pulling the piece from the kiln we have added extremely heavy reduction to bring out the full potential of copper and gold lustres.'

Their attitude to the progression of their work is summed up by Susan, who says:

'When Steven and I work together on our raku pieces we each try to go one step beyond what we already know. Perhaps the best advice that I received was from my graduate printmaking professor who told me that my job was to learn everything that I could learn from him and then go beyond: that is what Steven and I try to do.'

Opposite: 'Dream of a Fifteen Year Old', approximately $5\frac{1}{2} \times 5\frac{1}{2} \times 1\frac{1}{2}$ ft, 1985.

'Southern Lady', approximately $48 \times 18 \times 10$ inches, raku sculpture, 1985.

Technical information

The clay body which Steven has developed for large scale raku is:

30% Virginia kyanite (35 mesh) from the Kyanite Corporation, Dilwyn, Virginia, USA.
33% Cedar Heights GoldArt
33% Frederick fireclay
 4% wollastonite F1
    A trace of barium carbonate.

Steven and Susan have been doing raku for over sixteen years. In the beginning and for several years they lost 80% of everything that was made, mostly due to clay bodies which could not stand the shock of the procedure of raku or the scale they were imposing on it. Through extensive research and much trial and error on Steven's part he developed the Kemenyffy raku clay formula. Today their losses are negligible.

The white slip which Steven applies to sculptures and wall pieces before bringing them to Susan is intended to brighten the glazes and make the white in hands and faces more luminous and sparkling.

White slip formula
25% Edgar plastic kaolin
25% Kentucky ballclay
25% Custer feldspar
20% frit 3110
 5% barium carbonate

Opaque white glaze formula
30% Gerstley borate
30% frit 3110
25% Custer feldspar
 5% Edgar plastic kaolin
 5% barium carbonate
 1% tin oxide
 4% frit FL42

All glazes are applied at the same time, including the gold lustre.

Gold lustre formula
To the opaque white glaze formula the following is added:
$1\frac{1}{2}$% silver nitrate (crystals)
 1% yellow ochre pigment
 2% soda bicarbonate
$\frac{1}{2}$ of 1% Calgon water softener
After all the glazes have been dripped between the lines of the drawing the pieces are taken to the kiln room for the last procedure. Faces and hands of figures are roughly masked off with a cardboard template. A thin spray of dilute silver nitrate is wafted across the entire piece with an airbrush. The templates are removed and the wall pieces put (three at a time) vertically into the kiln.

Dilute silver nitrate spray formula
Using the above silver nitrate formula a textured substance comprising 20% 35 mesh kyanite or sand or grog, 20% frit FL42, and a trace of corn syrup is mixed and sprayed to add depth and drama to the pieces through texture and variegated colours.

Through the years the Kemenyffys have discovered the ideal reducing atmosphere for their images to be below the ground with cardboard (corrugated) acting as the source of smoke. The pieces are too large to fit into containers and the cardboard imparts a warm gray which is neither too insistent nor too diffuse.

Fiona Salazar

It was during her second year at the Royal College of Art, London, that Fiona Salazar began to formulate the ideas and techniques which shaped the way that her pots are presently formed and treated. At that time she felt the need to produce vessels which had an immediate visual impact and energy. This led her into the production of large coil-built pots, believing that by their sheer size and presence the pots would attain these qualities. Fiona had some success in achieving this, but she began to question her approach and to explore the possibilities of working in a smaller format, hoping still to retain the vital energy of the large coil pots. Many times her search for a direction led her to museums and galleries to study and draw the historic ceramics on view. Often the experience left her with a feeling of loss, trying to make sense of her own initiatives whilst being surrounded with the prolific results of past generations of potters who used so many different styles and techniques. During this period she was inspired by seeing pre-Dynastic Egyptian vessels, which led to the evolution of a whole personal philosophy and technique. Holding a small, black, burnished bottle and feeling the soft textural qualities that it shed became the catalyst which led to her work with low temperature burnished vessels.

All of Fiona's present work is centred on the concept of an enclosed form. The element of mystery within the confines of a clay vase or lidded vessel plays an important role in dictating both form and surface decoration.

She begins the forming process by throwing the bases of the vases and lidded jars. Starting with five or six thrown bases enables her to build up a series of vessels which will be worked upon as a group from inception to finish. Much of how a piece will develop in form and line is dictated by the initial 'lift' given to the base in the throwing process. The diameter and angle of the clay walls of the base will establish the fullness of form as the work grows. Fiona has no strictly controlled means of making the clay coils with which she builds the rest of the pot. She forms her coils by either rolling or squeezing the clay, and then attaches them to the thrown bases. Working on each base in turn enables the pots to dry off a little and the clay to stiffen, supporting

1 Fat coils of clay are added to the previously thrown clay base.

the next batch of coils. This method of coiling is an important part of her attitude to the work. The squeezing, rolling and attaching, the stretching and pulling of the clay and the gradual growth of the clay walls is all part of a slow, deliberate structuring of form which allows her the time and space to reflect upon each stage in the vessel's development.

At this point in the making process each piece begins to form a personality of its own. Areas of punctuation begin to emerge, full stops and flowing lines, and the relationship between the various elements of the vessel has to be taken into account. Some thought is now given as to which pieces are working harmoniously and which aren't and need to be rejected – though Fiona feels that lessons are learned from the rejected pieces as well as those she con-

tinues to work upon. She is continually searching for harmony – the relationship between the base and the fullness of the belly, judging the angle of shoulder and the balance of the neck and rim, constantly evaluating and adjusting the parameters within which each form is created.

Using a variety of found and made metal scrapers and wooden beaters, Fiona refines her forms as they grow slowly. Many of her scraping tools are fashioned in such a way as to enable awkward areas to be reached easily and refined – for example, the angle at which the neck joins the full shoulder of a flowing, fat-bellied pot. Working at eye level with the pot on a whirler gives Fiona the opportunity to monitor the progress of the pot's line and this assessment is helped by looking at the pot against a blank, white background.

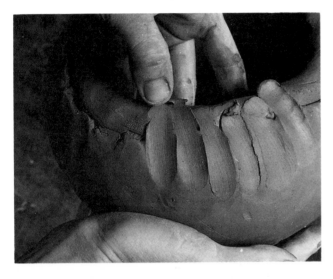

2 Above left: The pot progresses over a number of stages and each stage is allowed to stiffen slightly before any further weight of coils is added.

3 Below left: The form is refined by beating.

4 Above right: A metal kidney is used to refine the curvature of the neck.

During the latter stages of the forming process Fiona begins to concentrate on each piece individually and at this point she gives further consideration to the surface decoration. The relationship between colour and shapes is an integral part of the surface decoration of Fiona's burnished vessels. In the early stages of her present work she came into contact with Japanese woodblock prints of the Ukiyoye, one of the many styles that flourished during the Edo period in the 19th century. These prints, with their bold areas of colour and flattened perspective stimulated an emotional response and a set of ideas which later blossomed in her decorative motifs. When working out these ideas in two dimensions in her sketchbook Fiona is always aware that the sensuous curves of the pot will add another dimension to the design. Her early exploration of the forms and colours found in the Japanese prints saw the beginning of a deeper awareness of the relationships between form, line and colour. She takes and uses all types of visual information, from magazine articles to natural imagery, and draws upon these for inspiration.

Fiona's vessels have a conscious framework within which the decoration is carried out. The area from the base to shoulder, through to the neck and the rim and both the inside and outside of the pot are the boundaries within which the decorative symbols play their respective roles, carefully judged as to their balance and presence.

After the vessel has dried to a leatherhard state a ground is laid by spraying the pot with a terra sigillata slip, chosen because of its smooth, free-flowing quality and the density of the colour it produces. This fine particled slip is sprayed on to a depth sufficient to cover the surface of the pot evenly, taking care to control the thickness (too thin and the surface will appear patchy). When the pot is once again back to the leatherhard stage a number of tools are used to burnish the surface – the back of a metal spoon is the one most often used. Other tools are used for burnishing the awkward places – an agate-tipped gold leaf burnisher is used when working on the angle where the full curve of the shoulder and the wall of the neck meet. The burnishing is carried out once or twice until the surface of the terra sigillata is smooth and shiny.

5 After the pot has been sprayed with slip and allowed to dry slightly, the back of a spoon is used to burnish large areas. Other tools such as a pebble and an agate tipped tool are employed for smaller specific areas. Care must be taken not to burnish through the thin layer of slip.

'Black Vase', 11 inches.

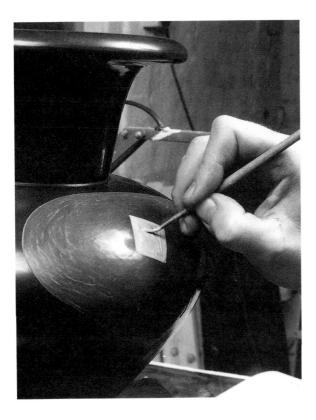

6 The motif is painted in slip upon the burnished surface. Care is taken to burnish each element of the motif separately.

7 Above right: Trying out a shape by using cut strips of paper.

8 Centre: Having decided the shape would work, Fiona paints on the motif.

9 Below right: Burnishing the motif using part of a manicure set.

After deciding on which colours she will use Fiona mixes glaze stains, body stains, metal oxides or a combination of all of these, with a base of liquid white ball clay. She mixes by eye rather than by weight or any other form of measurement, reinforcing her painterly approach. Using fine quality brushes the first marks are applied to the dense semi-reflective surface, using a bold freehand stroke – there is no room for hesitation. Once the mark has been made it cannot be successfully erased or taken off, so confidence is important when dealing with wet slips on burnished surfaces. When the shape of the motif is established the colour is blocked in. More than one coat may be required depending on the density of colour required. Some technical points have to be taken into account when burnishing colours which lie next to each other; the first level of colour needs to be leatherhard and burnished before any subsequent colours are added and any further colours must be treated similarly. After each piece is decorated it is allowed to dry out naturally.

Fiona uses a small toploading kiln to fire the pieces to their first temperature of Orton cone 09 (fired until the cone is flattened) around 950°C. Because of the way the vessels are constructed (clay coils joined onto a thrown base) a long slow firing is essential to minimise the chances of cracking, and the firing takes place over a period of 18 to 20 hours. When the pots are cool a low expansion frit glaze is used to glaze the inside of the vessels to the level of the base of the neck. The glaze is stained with a commercial coloured stain. The pots are then refired to Orton cone 09 again, when the glaze will mature.

The glaze becomes an important feature in the final quality of the pot. To peer into the vessel and see a well glazed, effectively coloured, shiny surface lends a finish and totality to the pot making process. The final stage is to warm the pot and apply polish to heighten the burnishing and bring the surface back to a state which is nearer to the soft sensuous quality gained during the first burnish when the pot was in the leatherhard stage.

Technical information

Terra sigillata
3500 centilitres of water
1500 grams white ball clay
  7.5 grams sodium hexameta phosphate (SHP)

Add clay and water together to allow to slake down. Grind SHP and add to slip, allow to stand for approximately 48 hours. Syphon off the top layer of water, then syphon off the top layer of fine clay particles in suspension. This fine particled slip can be coloured by the addition of commercial stains and oxides using percentage quantities or just by eye.

'Fish Handle Vase', $11\frac{1}{2}$ inches high.
Photography by John Coles.

Gallery

Ian Byers (UK)
Bowl, 16 inches in diameter,
decorated with coloured glazes,
raku fired to 960°C.

Gallery

David Roberts (UK)

Coil built raku bowl, 23 inches in diameter.
Below: Three coil built raku bottles; the
widest is 22 inches, the tallest 24 inches.

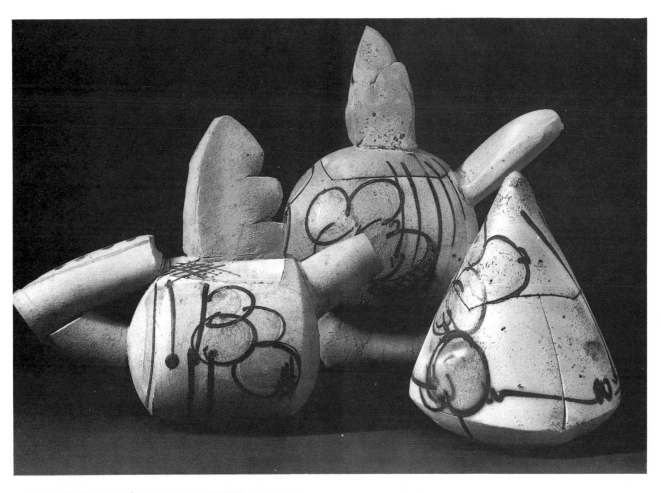

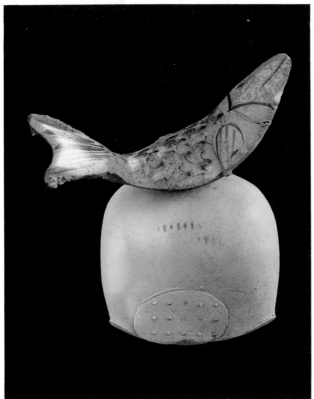

David Miller (UK)
Above: Three forms.

Fish sculpture, c. $12 \times 10\frac{1}{2}$ inches.

Ann Cummings (Canada)
'Fan Shaped Tray', $15 \times 13 \times 12\frac{1}{2}$ inches.
Raku fired slip, trailed and poured glaze.
(Photo: Paul Schwarz)

· 2 ·

Decorated earthenware

This chapter is concerned with earthenware and pots fired in the mid range of temperatures between 1000°C and 1200°C. The term earthenware is usually used to refer to pottery made of a porous fired body, sometimes covered in a glaze which offers a waterproof and cleanable surface. Glazes used in earthenware firings often contain lead oxide, and/or boric oxide, often fritted together. Sometimes the body itself is non-porous, fired to a high biscuit firing yet the covering glaze is fired within the lower temperatures of the earthenware range. Here I use the term in its broadest possible sense to include a range of different materials which can quite satisfactorily be categorised under the general term. Within this temperature range functional tableware is commonly made; more glazes are available and used than with low fired work, which means that the surfaces can be more easily cleaned. Within this group of makers we see a very marked interest in glazes, in applying them and seeing how they can be adapted, and a lot of surface decoration is carried out in coloured glazes, pigments and stains both under and over a glaze coating.

The work of Neil Ions is unglazed, though fired high enough to give strength and stability both to his sculptural pieces and his musical instruments; his designs still maintain a close link with the low fired burnished ware found in South American Indian cultures.

In the work Daphne Carnegy we see lively and colourful interpretations of floral and fruit motifs, painted over a bright, white tin-based glaze used over a warm red clay body. Stanley Mace Andersen uses similar materials and maintains a bright lively quality in his work, using bold splashes of direct colour. Roger Michell uses colour fluidly to create texture; he also highlights areas and sometimes includes humorous graphic images. Sometimes he airbrushes thin coloured glazes over the surface to tie together the various elements in a pot and give a sense of overall solidity. The work of Bill and Maureen Ellis shows how an airbrush can be used for the quality of line it can produce, resulting in strictly controlled design. Peter Meanley's work also illustrates strong, structured geometric patterns, where the finish has a dry or matt quality. David Taylor uses flowing glazes and pigments, capturing and holding the movement in the firing, creating considerable depth of colour and highlighting the textured surface. Tim Hodgkinson's dish also possesses a fluid textured quality, although this effect is conveyed by means of bold brushstrokes.

Patrick Loughran investigates both texture and colour and also introduces graphic images into his work. Flatter colours and simple motifs are characteristic of the tableware of both Anthony Phillips and Sabina Teuteberg, bright clean glazes with bold colours making for a cheerful range of functional pottery. These qualities need not be restricted to tableware – Jenny Orchard brings them to her flat wall piece.

Throughout all of the very diverse work featured in this chapter it's noticeable that bright colours and lively surfaces are prevalent. Whatever the influences which may be acting on the potters featured, whether their work has roots in Mediterranean folk wares, or factory products made during the Industrial Revolution, we see very strong, very personal explorations of ceramic decoration.

Bill & Maureen Ellis (USA)
Untitled vessel, (19 inches high × 19 inches wide).
Over a sanded biscuit fired surface, the design is masked out using graphic tape, contact paper and liquid latex. Multiple layers of underglaze colours are airbrushed onto the surface, and the masking materials are removed before firing to 1040°C.
(Photo: Michele Maier)

Roger Michell

Roger Michell's childhood visits to potters in the West Country became the first step upon a path that ultimately led to his present work – and he and his family now live and work in Cornwall. His early encounters with potters such as Bernard Leach, Harry Davis and Marianne de Trey left such a powerful impression on Roger that he became a helper in his spare time in the workshop of David Eeles. Roger's later studies at the Central School of Art and Design in London led to his spending a year with the sculptor Anthony Caro. Then Roger and his wife Danka Napoiorkowska decided to establish a pottery in north Yorkshire.

As they were interested in industrial methods of production, Danka and Roger developed a semi-industrial way of making slip castings on a production line basis. Their main ranges were lighthearted, slightly joky teasets; the walking teaset range typified the feel of the work that Danka was decorating and that Roger was designing and making in the 1970s. Danka and Roger maintained this industrial approach for about seven years, becoming immersed in questions of sales, effective production methods, low unit costs, etc. all of which accompany successful industrial practice.

Eventually the very success of the work that they were producing allowed Danka and Roger to indulge their otherwise neglected artistic feelings about form. Danka felt a need to return to printmaking (her primary discipline) and Roger wanted to reaffirm his position as an artist by controlling pieces of work through all the stages from conception to finish.

To fulfil these aims they moved to their present home and workshop in a beautiful part of Cornwall. Initially Roger felt that the refinding of himself as an artist would lie in the field of painting; however, critical self-assessment and a gradual awareness of his real abilities led him to acknowledge that studio pottery was the only way forward.

'I remember a saying by Ruskin, "Have nothing in your home which is not useful, and nothing in your house which you do not consider to be beautiful." I thought that to be a very significant idea, especially in that it is not a form-follows-function ideology, the idea that you can establish through the principle of function the ideal visual form – which is a powerfully held belief, almost a religion, rather that what it is, just an observation. I tend to follow the Ruskin idea – for me, considering the object beautiful is the most significant thing. Objects are accumulated through personal discretion and choice and that choice is one part of everybody's life that can be conducted with complete and utter freedom. There is not, and should not be, any dogma attached to what people choose to own for their own pleasure.'

With this philosophy as a starting point, Roger began to produce his new teasets. The skills learnt from the harsh disciplines of industry and the craftsmanship he has acquired allow him a freedom of expression to expand upon forms and decorative techniques. Last year's best-selling line is not important any more and his present work is motivated by what will make the piece successful, not by the unit cost. However, he still admires and is interested in industrial processes and innovative techniques, and to a small extent this interest is reflected in the way in which he produces his work today.

Roger is motivated by two main criteria when approaching any series of pots: one is that the work must be produced as well in technical terms as industry could produce it and the other is that the pots must be aesthetically pleasing in look, feel and concept.

A third criterion he often mentions is a need to break new ground with each new series of pots made, which was often not possible when working within commercial constraints. Roger feels that it is very important to be always on the edge of change, his work reflecting today's feelings and movements.

Roger's main interest is making teasets. He begins with a clear idea of what he requires from his pots, but this is invariably altered and modified as the pots take on an individuality and character all their own. This is encouraged by the open-minded attitude to development which Roger fosters; he allows the pots to be what they are without any of the burdens associated with a strong idealised statement.

'There has been a whole implication that the act of making pottery is somehow associated with a spiritual or political sense of right-mindedness – that is a very heavy burden for a teapot to bear.'

Teapot, c. 6 inches in height. Thrown and turned with pulled handle; spout rolled on a former and cut into six facets. Glaze is lead with additions of oxide, and the decorative effect is built up over two glaze firings, then overglazed with a thin coat of the same glaze which has a small addition of copper.

1 Above left: Using a sponge, colour is smeared and daubed freely and vigorously onto a biscuited pot.

2 Above right: The colour is progressively built up.

3 Left: The lid is given the same treatment prior to glazing and firing.

Through his teasets Roger can explore all sorts of human experiences; some of his shapes reflect certain human characteristics and foibles, such as pomposity, elegance of bearing or a round and comfortable figure. He sees his teasets as personal objects which have an intimate, human quality, being drawn from the china cabinet when guests appear or serving as an accompaniment to everyday living.

The other side of Roger's work, in considerable contrast to his teasets, is seen in his large-scale jars. They serve a different purpose – by their scale and nature they act as a

means of display, showing off wealth or affirming the owner's personality, as does choice of dress. Roger sees his large jars as vehicles through which people can express how they wish to be seen by others.

Almost all of Roger's present work is made by the thrown and turned method. The component parts of his teasets are treated firstly as individual units. When these are leatherhard, the foot rings and lid fittings are turned into them. At the same time, there is an initial refining of their form. The various items are assembled whilst still in the leatherhard stage. The assembled pots are then further turned and the whole surface refined to give the very smooth surface ideal for the style of decoration that Roger employs. Making forms from assembled units is an important element of Roger's work. He feels that he achieves a greater freedom of expression by the combination of smaller components and that any change in the direction and dynamics of profile and line is dictated by the choice of units. The use of assembly gives a relaxed feel to the final work.

Subtle historical references can be recognised in Roger's work, a crabstock handle or a Royal Worcester teapot shape, for instance. This may be an unconscious reference but Roger has an almost obsessive desire to make things, by using modern methods and materials, which are at least as good as those of the past. Although he makes his teasets in a precise manner, clues are purposely left to indicate how the piece was made – he may leave throwing rings on the inside of the work, or a line of slip where the teapot spout is attached to the body. This evidence is an indicator of the way in which Roger views other historical or contemporary work.

'One of the things that I like best about pottery is that you see the thing, pick it up, investigate it, find out how it works, and use the knowledge that you have to understand how it was made.'

Many of Roger's handles and spouts become decorative features in their own right. They may be made by a variety of methods: press moulded, thrown and turned, or rolled round formers. Roger does not always choose the most obviously efficient way to solve the problem of balancing additions such as handles and spouts because he makes his appendages for aesthetic as well as functional reasons. He regards these elements of his work in the same way that he assesses other objects which frame everyday activity: wine glasses, for instance, whose thin stems break all too easily if handled without proper care.

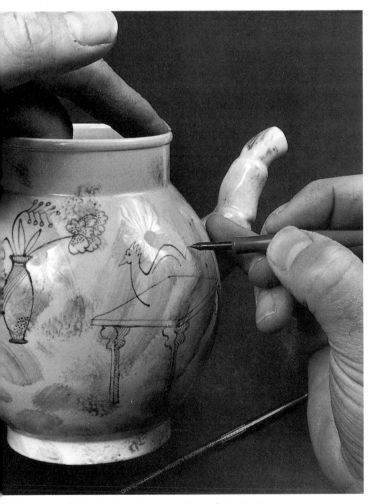

4 After the firing the sponged and daubed colours act as a background for further designs, which are initially drawn on the glaze in ink.

5 Enamel is applied with a brush using the ink as a guide.

'If people wanted to make wine drinking happen in the most efficient way then wine glasses would not have appeared. People do not want utensils that are wildly efficient, but they want to wrap up the act of using things in a kind of theatrical drama. I would suggest that the most efficient and convenient solution for picking up a teapot would resemble a bicycle handle bar grip. For me, one of the important aspects of using pottery is that one discovers a *way* of using it, by forming a kind of intimacy with the object and by somehow going out of one's way to find out the most comfortable way of using it. I believe people are extremely intelligent and ingenious and that they like finding out personal ways of doing things; I certainly do.'

After achieving the desired form and surface finish, Roger biscuit fires his work to a high temperature. The work is initially fired to a temperature of 1120°C and soaked for two hours. (The soak is critical to the achievement of the right silky vitreous surface, smooth enough for his decorative techniques.) If Roger is looking for a completely stain-free densely vitreous body then this initial firing is carried out to 1150°C/1160°C and soaked for two hours. (In this case also, the soak is critical because

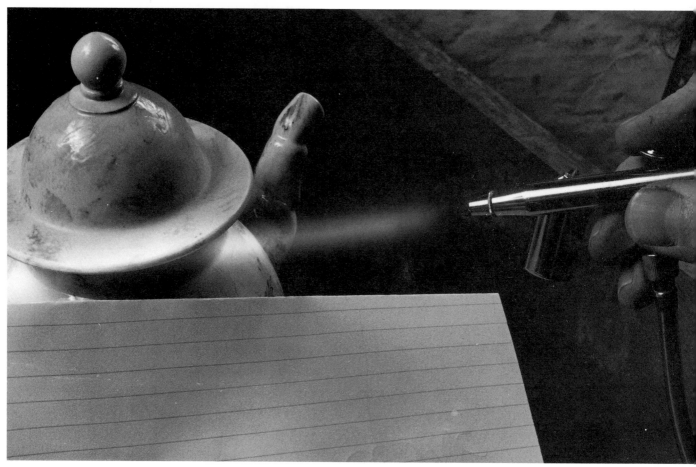

it prevents the glaze crazing after it has been fired on.) At the higher temperature there is a risk of his expressively cantilevered handles warping or moving, so Roger props these additions when he is setting the kiln.

After the high biscuit firing, Roger concentrates on the decoration. He usually begins with the application of underglaze colours. They are mixed with a solution of gum arabic to prevent smudging when the pots are being packed into the kiln or similarly handled. Roger employs a number of techniques when applying the underglaze colour, one of which is to use various types of masking medium such as Copydex. These he applies in a number of ways – stroking the surface of the pot with a feather loaded with masking fluid is one of the more unusual techniques. Underglaze colours may be banded in lines upon the surface of the pot or colour may be sponged on, sprayed and spattered to give a stippled effect or even applied and then taken off with a rubber eraser which leaves a slight graining of the pot's surface. The primary concern in these early applications of colour is to explore ways of enhancing the visual surface texture.

'The object determines its own decorative success. I do not set out with a pattern and technique and then decorate the pot, but I start with various materials and tools and with the knowledge that I want to achieve a certain effect and then I proceed to build slowly upon that.'

When Roger is happy with the effect created by underglaze colour, he will harden on the colour by firing the piece to 1000°C. If this is not done, the powdery surface of the underglaze colour will cause the transparent glaze which follows to crawl and pull away from the decoration. Two basic glazes are used: a low-solubility alkaline glaze and a lead bisilicate glaze, both transparent. The low-solubility alkaline glaze is fired to maturity at 1040°C with a two hour soak; the lead glaze is fired to 1080°C without the soak. Both glazes are applied to the pot by spraying.

Some of the lead glazed pieces are decorated by overlaying coloured glazes upon the initial transparent glaze coating. These coloured glazes are generally made by the addition of oxides to the transparent base glaze. Four basic colours are used; each colour is line blended until three tonal values are achieved for each separate colour.

6 Opposite page, above: Latex is applied as a resist medium prior to airbrushing the surface.

7 Opposite page, below: A thin overglaze colour is sprayed over the whole of the pot.

8 Left: The latex is removed after spraying and prior to firing.

These colours are dripped, trailed and poured over the shoulders of pots and allowed to run into each other in order to create texture within the colour. The technique of alternating glazing with firing may be repeated many times before Roger is happy that he has achieved the desired effect. The very last firing is done with the application of a slightly coloured glaze over the whole surface of the pot, almost like a wash in watercolour painting. Roger also uses overglaze enamels and lustres in his work.

Although he is primarily concerned with visual texture, a sense of fun is never far away in Roger's work. He will often draw pots upon his pots – occasionally scenes from his own home and life appear on his jars. Roger is concerned that pots should not be the vehicles for any heavy messages. He is as much concerned with the mystery of surface decoration as he is with the techniques that achieve it. His highly individual approach means that he may regard an average of 1 in 6 of the pieces that are finally finished as failures – these are not failures by any technical criteria but they fail to satisfy Roger sufficiently.

Technical information

Clay
White plastic earthenware (British Industrial Sands)

Clear lead glaze
80% lead bisilicate
20% cornish stone
small addition of china clay
Glaze fired to 1080°C without a soak.

Low-solubility alkaline glaze
Very bright quality industrial frit glaze, code no. J.C. 983, purchased in powder form.
Glaze fired to 1040°C with a two hour soak.

Sugar is added to the glazes to help them stick to the surface of the high biscuit fired vitreous earthenware; the sugar also helps to form a hard surface which is easier to handle during kiln packing.

Underglaze colour
Purchased from Blythe Colours, Stoke-on-Trent

Opposite: Decorated jar, 13–14 inches high. Thrown and turned. Sponged underglaze is hardened on, then glazed with low solubility glaze and decorated with pen and enamel. The jar was fired and then airbrushed with blue enamel, using Copydex resist.

Photography by John Coles.

Neil Ions

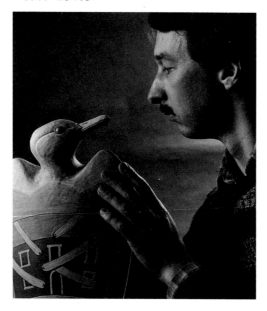

During childhood Neil Ions was interested in the craft of construction and developed a serious interest in ornithology which was to influence him in later life. At the local art school, his keen enquiring mind motivated him to try his hand at many skills, ranging from pottery to silversmithing.

Neil moved to Newport College of Art, South Wales, where he intended to train as a painter, but decided to work instead in the sculpture department. His three-dimensional work there consisted mainly of objects that combined ceramics with wood and metal. And his figurative work began at Newport, albeit in a tentative, minimal way.

It was also at Newport that Neil first took an interest in American Indian art and artifacts, an interest that he still maintains. This was initially a purely gut response to the shapes and forms seen within Aztec and Mayan architecture and led to a desire to translate these images into contemporary sculpture. The first sculptural work at Newport was based on a reworked image of the Temple of Jaguars in Mexico but Neil changed the deities depicted there from the original animals to motor cars, portraying the automobile as the god.

A growing satisfaction in the manipulation of clay experienced in his final weeks at Newport kindled in Neil a desire to direct his efforts primarily towards ceramics.

At the Royal College of Art, London, Neil continued his sculptural work but began to look at a lot more pottery made by the American Indians, such as the stirrup-handled vessels from Peru. He began to make direct copies of these

pots in order to understand them better, learning the techniques of form and decoration necessary to make them. He therefore began to acquire the techniques of slip painting and an understanding of firing temperatures which formed the basis of his work today.

Pursuing his interest in American Indian work, Neil visited the British Museum to see an exhibition of Mayan pottery. Amongst the exhibits were fragments of whistles and one ocarina, which greatly excited Neil. After making a few sketches and trial-and-error experiments he managed to produce a clay instrument that worked.

Although sculptural work continued the musical instruments became an increasingly important sideline which slowly began to take over Neil's full attention. He began to look at flutes, tin whistles and recorders, trying to understand how the various musical mechanisms worked and how to interpret them in clay. Neil's love of music allowed him to enjoy fully the delights of producing successful pleasing notes and tones from his ceramic musical instruments. Initially these instruments were simple in design as Neil had little information on which to base his work apart from vague references to Greek Pan pipes, etc.; he had to find his own solutions.

Neil's final show at the Royal College consisted of 50% musical instruments and 50% pots, the interest in sculptural work having for the moment subsided. Most of the pots were vase forms and coiled vessels with stylised motifs painted on them.

Gradually this period of vase and vessel making laid the

foundation of Neil's present sculptural work. The change in emphasis back from vessels to sculpture began in November 1975 when Neil became a founder member of group workshops established at Stow on the Wold, Gloucestershire. He spent six years at these workshops almost exclusively devoted to developing his musical instruments, with periodic excursions into vessel and sculpture making. In 1981 Neil established his present workshop in Kitebrook, Gloucestershire, where his work consists of large three-dimensional sculptural pieces, ocarinas and flutes.

The main sources of inspiration in Neil's work are to be found in conservation—the welfare of wildlife and habitats. His studies in ornithology as a young boy gave him a deep-rooted knowledge of bird forms, and their plumage. His involvement in the Friends of the Earth movement arms him with a passion to express the plight facing our wildlife. Many ideas that inspire the larger pieces may have been lying around in Neil's mind for a long time before being translated into a three-dimensional object. The ideas may take the form of a couple of lines of poetry, a song or a single photograph.

The whale motif was introduced into Neil's work after he saw a film of divers swimming with whales in a pool. A flautist was playing at the side of the pool and eventually the whale began to imitate the sound of the flute through its blow-hole until the same pitch was achieved. Neil felt this to be a genuine attempt at imitation. He wanted to translate what to him was a magical event into the surface decoration of a pot. Initially his attempts took the form of stylised and flat two-dimensional paintings; later he was to develop the whale image into three-dimensional objects. This development was prompted by another found visual image, a photograph of two Baluga white whales rolling over each other in a courtship posture. Neil took this image and made a twin ocarina showing stylised humpback whales (changing the species gave Neil greater scope for

Tern sculpture with fledgling ocarinas, 15 inches long. Slabbed and coiled.

tonal, textural and colour combinations). This twin instrument was designed to be played by two people cheek to cheek, which gave an intimate quality to an intimate subject; other subjects such as turtle doves have been used similarly.

Not having trained as a craft potter (in the broadest sense), Neil adopts a simple low technology approach to the production of his work. His large pieces begin as press-moulded dish shapes which can be combined or used singly, and simple slabbed forms. These basic shapes are altered by cutting or distortion – it depends on how the piece is to be developed.

The small bird ocarinas begin as two pieces from an egg-shaped press mould; the rest of the form is free modelled which allows Neil to stylise and emphasise attributes as the work grows and develops. Low relief for wing tips or slabs, coiling for tails and necks, etc. are added as required.

Pipes for flutes are all extruded. Within the construction of the flutes and sculptural forms Neil uses devices for strengthening otherwise weak areas even if these devices are more functional than realistic. (For example, he joins wing tips on his bird forms.) The holes on ocarinas and flutes are built up for strength which makes for better display and stability. The raised holes are visual as well as practical features, acting as focal points round which to start the painted surface decoration.

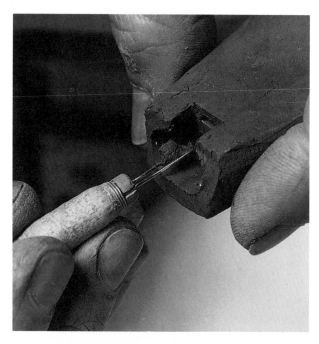

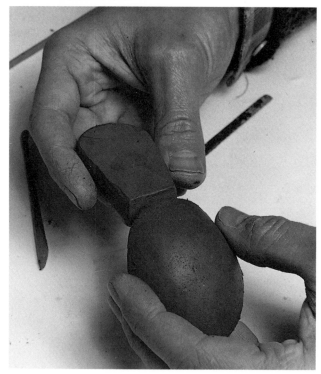

1 Opposite page, above left: From the back of a previously made bird form an ovoid is cut and remade into a concave shape and refitted.

2 Opposite, below left: Two press-moulded halves of an ocarina are attached together.

3 Opposite, above right: The mouthpiece of the ocarina is formed.

4 Opposite, below left: Joining the mouthpiece to the body of the ocarina forming the tail of a stylised bird.

5 Below: Adjusting the mouthpiece to give an accurate sound (the pitch increases as the piece dries).

6 Below: Forming the wings of the bird ocarina.

7 Right: Testing the ocarina for an accurate fit.

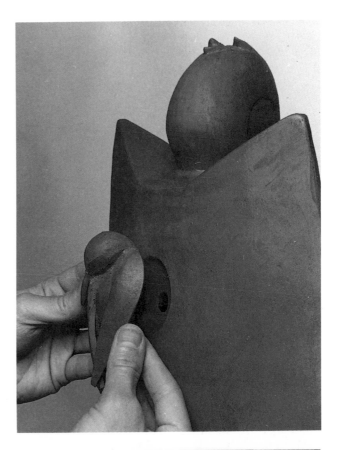

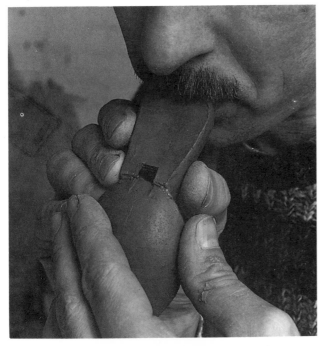

Detail of completed ocarina attached to the sculpture.

Bridges are made to span the width between double flutes in order to add strength and a further focus for surface decoration. Often these bridges take the form of stylised fish, frogs, lizards, otters and other creatures. These are painted or modelled in low relief on flat pieces of clay or they are full three-dimensional forms. The majority are a combination of all these techniques. Such features are often found in the artifacts of the American Indian.

1 Above: A design is sketched on to the clay figure of a bird.

2 Below: Background colour is applied.

3 Right: The border is highlighted with contrasting colour.

Opposite: Cormorant sculpture with chough ocarina attached, 18 inches high. Slabbed, with some coiling. Back view shown here: front on p. 49.

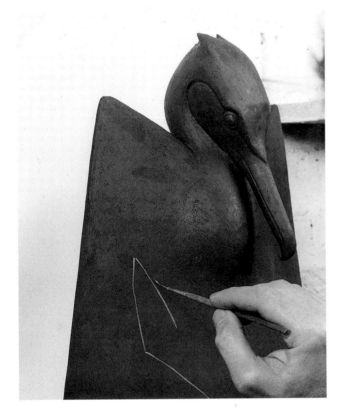

Neil's large sculptural pieces generally consist of one main three-dimensional form with inter-related decoration constructed or painted upon it. The images that form the decoration come from the natural environment, and species are chosen for their inter-relationship — for instance, sea birds and seals may be chosen, or frogs and fish. These images are then combined aesthetically to present a sensitive balance of contour and colour. This may require a degree of stylisation or distortion. Neil feels a need to consider both natural relationships and artistic form. He does not arbitrarily throw elements together if there is no relationship between them and if they cannot satisfactorily combine in terms of form, line and colour. Often within a larger work an ocarina will be found which can be lifted off and played; this establishes a bond between the piece and the observer and extends the idea of inter-relationship between species. 'In nature everything is related and there is a need to see the whole picture; you cannot isolate species from each other. I see it as an aesthetic challenge to incorporate such diverse visual elements successfully.'

Much of Neil's inspiration for pattern comes directly from nature but his work is stylised. For example, he does not directly copy, say, the feathers of a bird or the pelt of a creature: rather he builds up short and long brushstrokes, lines and dots which give an overall textural and tonal quality which immediately evokes feathers or pelt. This stylisation is important for Neil as he feels that the pieces he makes should not be regarded as imitations of natural forms. Colours are chosen and are loosely related to the tonal and primary values of colour found in the natural environment and to the subject under scrutiny. This stylisation of colour can also be seen in the American Indian artifacts that Neil so much admires. He stylises in order to give himself the freedom to use colour intuitively, without any formal constraints. However, he does consider certain qualities, such as fixed tonal values, before embarking upon any painted decoration.

4 Below: Stylised details are applied to the central motif.

5 Right: A dark pigment is used to highlight the completed design.

Opposite: Cormorant sculpture with chough ocarina attached.

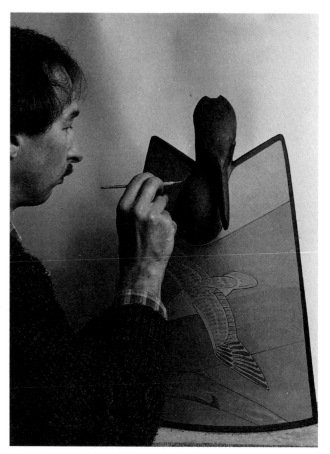

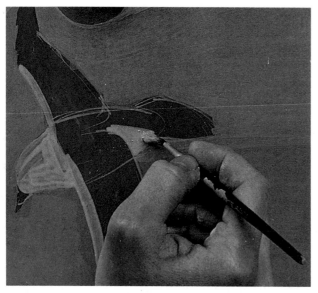

For surface decoration, Neil applies a layer of base slip, painting it on with squirrel lining brushes. He then draws on the linear patterning which will contain further slip colours. This patterning can follow an entirely abstract path or can be a figurative stylisation of plumage or form. The pigment used for outlining the pattern is of a dark rich brown colour, a mixture of manganese oxide with red earthenware clay. Occasionally a yellow or white outline is painted over the brown pigment to produce a contrasting line. Once the pattern is established, slips of various colours are painted within the delineated areas.

One, two or three coats of slip are applied according to the density of colour required, paler colours needing more coats. Neil usually works with a palette of around twenty colours and shades and he knows the depth of each colour by experience. He allows the slip to fall from the brush rather than painting it onto the surface of the piece; this action prevents the brush from breaking the surface of the previous, slightly stiffened coating. Otherwise the dark colour of the base clay would show through. After the areas of colour have been blocked in, the outlines are repeated with the dark brown pigment.

When the work is touch dry, the pieces are burnished to varying degrees with the burnishing tools used for jewellery, dental tools or custom-made forged steel tools.

Neil's early style of pottery painting, which imitated American Indian artifacts (particularly the Nazca pots) produced a very flat dense colour with a dark outline and a burnished finish. He burnishes, not very highly, following the lines of the decoration to reduce smudging, but more recently he has been less interested in burnishing strongly and favours a more textured semi-matte finish to the work. This he achieves by seeding the commercial body stains which are used to stain his slips with oxides of copper, cobalt, iron, chrome, etc. This gives the slips a more visual and tactile texture, the metal oxides being coarser in quality than the stains. Often Neil uses the flatter colour and textured colour in combination to support each other. However, without any burnishing at all the surface becomes dry and gritty in feel, so a light burnish is used to produce the silky, satin finish more sympathetic to the touch.

Neil fires his work in an oxidising atmosphere to a temperature of 1080°C, a deliberate increase in temperature from that of most burnished slipware. This increase in temperature improves durability while still preserving the colours and refined surface. After the firing and while still warm, pieces are polished with a silicon product which soaks into the porous surface of the work. This enhances the light burnish and facilitates cleaning.

From beginnings which spanned vessel making, musical instruments and some sculpture, Neil's current preoccupation is his larger pieces of sculpture which reflect his involvement with questions of the environment and nature, and with man's relationship with his fellow creatures. Through his work, Neil hopes that people will recognise and share the concern that he feels for the environment but, primarily, he wants them to enjoy all his ceramics as works of art.

Photography by John Coles.

Technical information

Clay
50% St Thomas white stoneware
50% red earthenware (Potclays)

Slip
Basic powdered white earthenware (Pottery Crafts) mixed into liquid form. Stains and oxides are added (strength is estimated from experience) and all is sieved through a 200 mesh sieve. This chef-like approach allows for a certain amount of accident. Neil uses 20 colours and shades at any one time and has had to learn by trial and error how to assess and alter them.

Daphne Carnegy

Since 1980 Daphne Carnegy has worked from the Kingsgate workshop complex in north London, producing a range of maiolica painted domestic tableware. Like many potters, Daphne's introduction to clay was at an adult education class run by the local education authority. In 1976, whilst she was living in France, she became apprenticed to a faïence potter in the Burgundy region. The production basis of the French pottery influenced Daphne, encouraging her love of throwing and domestic pottery, and her exploration of form and shape began at this time.

In 1978 Daphne came to a difficult decision and left France to attend the studio ceramics course at Harrow College of Higher Education, near London. This decision stemmed from her need to gain a broader knowledge of ceramics and to pursue areas of pottery making she had not yet touched on. She knew the reputation that Harrow had for teaching throwing and the production of domestic ware, and this approach appealed to her.

Her choice of producing tin glazed, maiolica painted domestic pottery was to some extent influenced by the previous work she had done with the faïence potter in France and also the research she had done at college on the production and decoration of Italian arbarellos (decorated drug jars). The 14th century faïence drug jar became Daphne's first serious encounter with the challenges of brushwork and the various problems that in-glaze painting can create. Since then Daphne has built up a repertoire of shapes and forms, brushstrokes and motifs dealing with things she finds interesting in the world around her. She is a keen gardener, and the flowing lines and bright colours of her flower beds and the fat full shapes of apples feature predominantly in her recent maiolica work. Tin glazed maiolica is perfectly suited to Daphne's interests as a potter. The tin glaze fires white when applied over the warm red earthenware, so the floral motifs, directly painted on the glaze, glow with a soft warmth, reminiscent of the simple Mediterranean peasant wares that she so much admires.

1 Dipping the biscuited pot in the white glaze.

Decisions about the colour and surface quality are made in the earliest stages, beginning with the choice of earthenware clays used to give a variety and range of colour densities. By mixing two clays together (buff clay and red earthenware clay) Daphne achieves the warm apricot colour which is found in the folk pottery of many Mediterranean regions. It is important to achieve the right balance between buff and red clay, as a significant aspect of the finished work is the contrast between the white, bright, reflective shiny glazed surface and the warm, soft bare clay which is revealed on the underside of plates and the unglazed foot rings of the bowls. The overall effect of the two clays is to evoke white, sun-bleached walls and the soft warm ochre earth surrounding them. This quality is further enhanced in the finished pieces by the floral overpainting of warm greens and blues, which are bright and sunny with flowing lines.

When deciding on the forms which are going to be made, consideration is given to the way in which the decoration will fit upon the pot's surface. Although Daphne uses a metal rib to smooth and flatten the surface during the throwing process, she has increasingly begun to leave some slight indication or clue to the way in which the fingers and knuckles are used in the making of the pot—not too exaggerated, which would interfere with the smooth flow of the brush over the surface, but just enough to break the possible monotony of the blank surface.

All Daphne's forms have evolved through various stages; her aim is to achieve a simple, functional, strong shape which will carry her bold decoration. Allowing the

form to grow in a fluid manner gives greater scope and freedom for the bold brushstrokes used to decorate the surface. A conscious effort is made to avoid defining too rigidly any change in direction the pot may take – for example, where the belly of a jug changes in shape and direction as it merges into the neck of the jug is an area which can be strongly defined and may act as a border or as part of a framework where decorative motifs can be infilled. Daphne, however, allows her forms to flow from one element to another with the minimum of definition, which gives her the freedom at the painting stage to redefine parts of the pot's body, neck, lip, etc. and to allow the decorative motifs to flow over and through the changes in direction of the pot's form. Increasingly her forms have become a vehicle for decoration, with direct and simple pot making.

'I would rather define areas by brushwork than have restrictions placed upon the decoration by some sort of predefinition of the form during the throwing process.'

Appendages such as handles are treated as simply and directly as possible; they are either extruded or pulled in a quick, straightforward manner. On some occasions slips are applied to the rims of pots which may otherwise be awkward to paint or band with one-stroke, direct brushstrokes at the overglaze stage. The glaze has a high quantity of tin oxide which acts an an opacifier; this modifies the colours of the slipped areas, lying under the glaze, making them muted and misty. The slip therefore needs to have enough strength in the oxides to show through the opaque qualities of the glaze.

When a batch of work is made and thoroughly dried a kiln is packed and fired to approximately 970°C. When the pots are cooled and unpacked the kiln's load is glazed as a batch. Dipping is the method used, which offers a good surface on which to paint – if the glaze were sprayed small dots of glaze would be left on the surface which would interfere with the smooth flow of the pigment over the pot's surface. The thickness of the glaze is crucial to the surface quality; if it is too thin the red earthenware body shows through, giving a patchy look. Daphne finds that it is possible to leave the work for up to two days before the glazed surface of the pot becomes too powdery to paint the pigment on in a free-flowing manner. This is sufficient time to allow her to decorate a batch of work in one session.

The brushes used are all one-stroke pencil shaders, liners and flat shaders, made of nylon to promote a good, springy, slightly resilient feel in the brush; in general the script liners are used to outline the motifs and the one-stroke flat shaders are used for the larger, broader areas of

2 The foot ring has been waxed to resist the glaze.

51

colour. Daphne taught herself to use the brushes and has a thorough knowledge of what effect each can create.

In her earlier work, Daphne applied the motifs in a comparatively rigid way; the pot was divided in a grid-like pattern which created panels where the motifs could be painted in. But as we have just seen, with the kind of forms she is now making the lines and motifs are applied in a more free-flowing, organic spirit, though she still retains the option of using a brushed line to define a framework. Drawing plays an important part in her approach to decoration, though she feels that the task of painting a two-dimensional idea on to a three-dimensional object will often modify and change an idea. She feels that only a certain number of her ideas can ever be translated into tangible objects, yet she still finds that looking and as-

similating is a constant process, and sketching on pots or paper is very important to her.

Daphne uses standard metal oxides and some commercial stains to give her the colour palette she needs. By intermixing oxides and stains many subtle variations can be achieved. Some stains are more refractory than others and a little glaze is added to these to help flux the pigment, otherwise the stain will lie upon the surface of the fired and cooled glaze. Most of the fluxing oxides are mixed with china clay to 'carry' the pigment and to help counteract running. The colours are sieved and used as one would use watercolours – mixing the correct consistency by the eye – and colours can also be intermixed before application. At any one time Daphne employs approximately six different colours or colour combinations in her decoration.

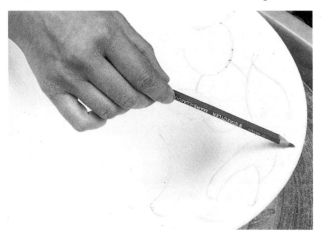

3 The design is freely drawn on the pot in light pencil.

4 A light lemon underglaze colour is brushed on as a background.

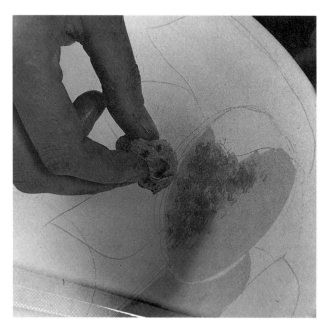

5 Orange, red and green colours are sponged on.

6 Using a royal blue colour the leaves are highlighted thinly with one stroke.

Detail of surface decoration.

7 The design is outlined in a dense dark blue pigment.

Using the wider and larger brushes, firstly the paler colours are painted on in broad full strokes and then outlined with the stronger pigments using the liner brushes until a flowing decoration grows upon the surface of the pot. Small, brightly coloured jewel-like dots are strategically placed to focus the eye upon certain elements within the decoration.

Daphne also uses a stippling technique on apples and other fruits, or full, round motifs. Firstly a wash of yellow is laid down to define the basic, plump shape of the fruit and over this a variety of other pigments, green, yellow, red etc. are sponged on to create a stipple effect and build up layers of subtle colours. Tonal qualities of the colours are used to suggest the fullness of the fruit. Daphne draws upon a wide range of background material for her imagery, including the paintings of Cézanne and Matisse and particularly the watercolours of Gauguin. Architectural themes also play a part in her work, and her deceptively simple bold line is thoughtfully derived from a wealth of sources.

During the glaze firing the oxides and stains react with the tin and zinc in the glaze, subtly breaking up the surface of the drawn line, and bleeding of the oxides can occur which fuzzes the outlines and flows through the glaze. Copper oxide is inclined to behave like this and the addition of nickel oxide can help to stabilise it. The reaction with the glaze is caused partly by the fluidity and movement of the molten glaze and the fusion between the pigment and the glaze when fired to Orton cone 01. Daphne's knowledge of her materials and their reactive qualities is used to good effect in developing colour combinations and in pushing her palette further.

Staying with a strong body of motifs, refining, initiating and working through new ideas has seen a slow, evolutionary change within Daphne's work. Her first trip to Italy to see early maiolica ware was also her first step to a simple, bold approach to decoration and moving along that road has to led to pottery with a bright, sunny quality, colourful and strong.

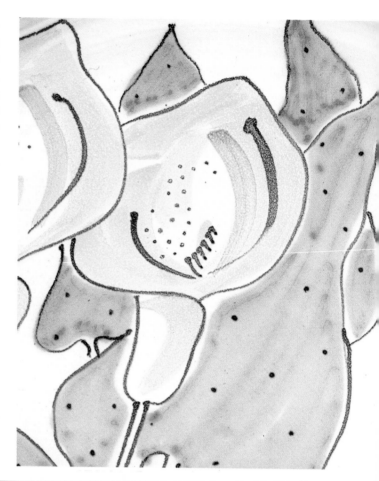

Technical information

Maiolica glaze

60% lead bisilicate
9% borax frit
15% cornish stone
6% china clay
8% tin
5% zircon
2% zinc
2% bentonite

Maiolica colours

Liner colours

dark blue liner
1 part cobalt oxide
$\frac{1}{4}$ part nickel oxide
$\frac{1}{2}$ part china clay

black/brown
2 parts iron oxide
1 part nickel oxide
1 part china clay

Filler colours

purple/blue
2 parts manganese oxides
1 part cobalt oxide
3 parts china clay

yellow/ochre
1 part rutile
1 part lead bisilicate

leaf green
2 parts rutile
1 part copper oxide

grey/blue
1 part rutile
1 part cobalt oxide

orange/rust
1 part iron oxide
3 parts rutile
1 part lead bisilicate

mushroom
2 parts manganese
3 parts rutile

'Lidded jar – irises', 14 inches high. Tin/zircon glaze with painted in-glaze decoration using oxides and underglaze colours.

Opposite: Detail of surface decoration.

Opposite: 'Large bowl – tomatoes, lemons and olives', 14 inches diameter. Tin/zircon glaze with painted and sponged in-glaze decoration (using oxides and underglaze colours).

Photography by John Coles.

Gallery

Jenny Orchard (Australia)
Right: Two vases.
Below: 'Celebration', 1985, wall plaque made in
collaboration with Robyn Jordon. 4 ft × 8 ft,
earthenware; uses commercial underglazes.

Stanley Mace Andersen (USA)
Casserole dishes. Earthenware,
maiolica, using brushwork.
(Photo: A. Hawthorne)

Sabina Teuteberg (Switzerland)
From a rolled slab of coloured clay the
forms are jiggered and jolleyed over
moulds to produce a range of
earthenware tableware.
(Photo: Roland Aellig)

Anthony Phillips (UK)
Soup bowls, 7 inches diameter.
Slip decorated on red earthenware.

Gallery

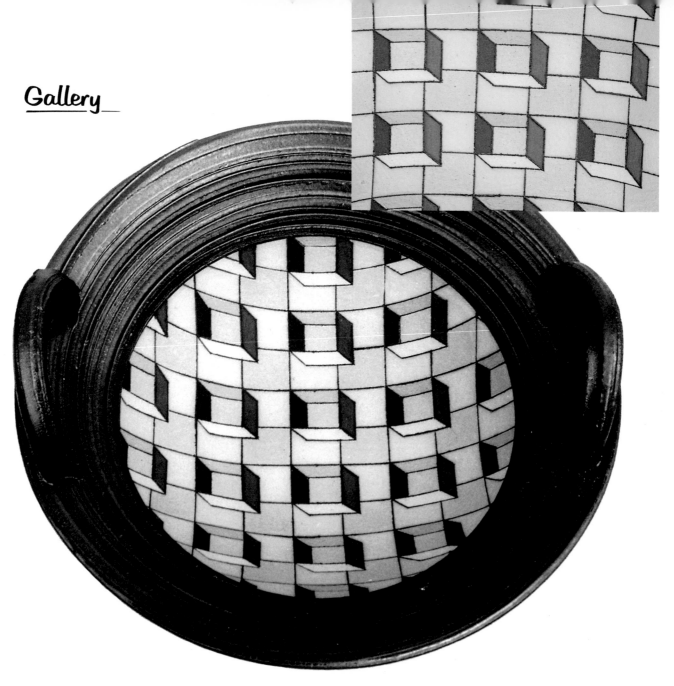

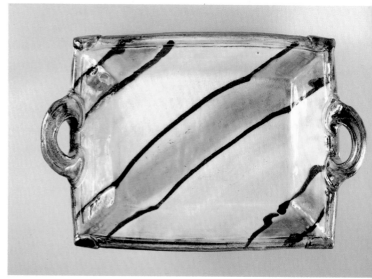

Peter Meanley (UK)
Above: Bowl, constructed from separate components of 50% T.
material and 50% St Thomas oxidising clay. The central motif is
incised, dried and biscuit fired to 1030°C. A high manganese and
copper glaze is rubbed into the drawn lines and cleaned off the rest
with a sponge. The centre of the bowl is waxed to resist the glaze
poured on the rim. The glaze is hardened on at 1110°C and slips are
painted on the centre. These may also be 'hardened on' once or twice
to 1110°C. The final firing occurs at 1190°C.

Tim Hodgkinson (UK)
Right: Square Dish. Slip and glaze decoration using copper,
manganese and iron, borax glaze fired to 1120°C.

David Taylor (Canada)
Vase, 24 inches high.
Cone 03 biscuit 900–950°C glaze.
Combination of thrown and slab built
parts; foot and body are thrown
separately and attached. The body is
adjusted to form an oval at the top. A
hump moulded slab is attached to the
body. The top is thrown and attached
to the shoulder, the handles are
thrown as open cylinders. White slip
is sprayed or brushed over the
surface, plus purple and black
underglazes. Two batches of glaze are
used – one with 2% copper carbonate
for bright Egyptian blue, the other
transparent. Potassium dichromate
lightly brushed over copper carbonate
give chartreuse, brushed over
transparent gives acid yellow. Cobalt
gives dark blue-black. The glaze is
free flowing carrying the colour with
it, being picked up and channelled by
the sgraffito marks.

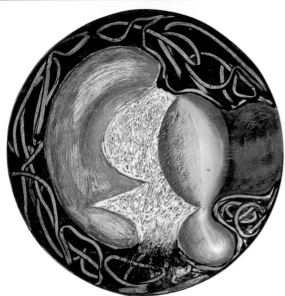

Patrick Loughran (USA)
Untitled plate, 24 inches wide × $3\frac{1}{2}$ inches high.
Glazed earthenware.

· 3 ·

Stoneware and porcelain

In this chapter we move on to stoneware, porcelain and other vitrified clays all of which are fired within the region of 1200°C to 1300°C. Very few commercially viable clays will maintain any useful form when fired at temperatures in excess of 1350°C, for studio ceramics at least. The particular qualities of high fired work are a hard, dense vitrified body, with a close cohesion between clay and glaze. Historically, a tradition in high fired work has often been established when a culture develops the kiln technology for attaining the necessary temperatures. Today our equipment is sufficiently sophisticated to allow high temperature work to be carried out in almost any small workshop.

Traditionally, subtle colours and effects have been created by high firing techniques such as reduction firing. Here oxygen is reduced from the atmosphere of the firing chamber at certain points in the firing cycles, which affects the molecular structure of any oxides contained within the clay and glaze; this subsequently determines the colour of the fired pots. Such subtleties in colours were previously denied to potters using oxidised firings (usually associated with electric kilns) where the atmosphere in the firing chamber remains constant. Recently, however, a broad range of stable colour pigments has been made available

which enable potters using both reduction and oxidised firings to achieve a wide variety of colours, both vibrant and more restrained.

Much of the work featured in this chapter makes use of these developments in colour technology. An exception is the work of Eric James Mellon; he creates lyrical graphic images on the surface of his pots by drawing directly on to his biscuit fired ware, using wood ash based glazes and metal oxides. Andrew McGarva's vessels also rely upon sensitive graphic qualities for their impact. Tom and Elaine Coleman use a simple celadon glaze to highlight the intricate carvings on the surface of their pots; the detail is variously defined by the different thickness of the glaze covering, so that the colour appears to shift.

My own work is featured in this chapter; in my case, and to some extent in the work of Clive Davies, John Glick and David Scott, visual texture is created by the multiple applications of coloured slips, glazes, stains and oxides, using a variety of techniques to obtain a richly patterned surface. John Maltby, Archie McCall and Dorothy Hafner all use shapes and colours in a very vivid, idiosyncratic way, creating strong and personal work. Angela Verdon's pierced vessels show great clarity and poise.

The work of Dorothy Feibleman is intricate in colour and construction; generally small in scale, her work is beautifully poised and balanced, and the pots by Curtis and Susan Benzle possess something of those qualities, too.

Curtis & Susan Benzle (USA)
'Blade', inlaid coloured porcelain and incising millefiori technique, and slip painting.

John Gibson

I didn't begin by making a conscious decision to become a potter – this grew out of the circumstances I found myself in. To start with, I wanted something to alleviate the crushing boredom of a factory job, and pottery classes looked as if they might be more entertaining than the usual courses listed at the local colleges of further education. I became increasingly dissatisfied with my lot as a factory worker, and felt I would have to make a choice between full-time employment in the factory, or try and make a career as a potter. After two years at evening classes, I was passionate enough about ceramics for the decision to be made for me – all I needed was to find a suitable full-time course in studio ceramics. I was lucky in living within easy travelling distance of Chesterfield College of Art and Design, which ran a course I was particularly interested in – and I enrolled in 1975.

During the next three years I found that saltglaze techniques played a very important part in the development of my work. At that time, I relied heavily on the properties of fire, flame and kiln atmosphere to give me the richness of decorative effect I wanted. The seductive qualities of surface colour and depth of texture which salt vapour gave to the pots was a never-ending source of excitement and interest to me. Using the flame to alter and transmit the salt vapour through and around the pots, the kiln itself became an important tool through which to decorate my work.

Towards the end of my time at college, circumstances arose which were to directly affect the whole way I approached the design and decoration of my work. My fel-

low student, Josie Walter, obtained the lease on an old coaching inn situated in the nearby Victorian spa town of Matlock. I was invited to help restore the building and work in the Courtyard pottery, and this I did, when my college course finished.

But this move presented me with a dilemma – the workshop was established in the centre of a large town, where there was neither the space nor a suitable environment for building a kiln for the production of saltglaze tableware. An electric kiln was the only kiln suited to the location and the quiet garden atmosphere of our courtyard studio and shop. So, I was forced to alter fundamentally my outlook – gone was the gift of flame which had held such an important place in the decoration of my previous work.

What had my new surroundings to offer me? Initially I felt restricted by the new location, but given the parameters I had to work within, I felt I must decide what were the essential qualities of work fired in an electric kiln, and develop my own work from there.

I chose to use a dense, white firing, vitrified clay, it being best suited for carrying colours, and I had already had some experience in the manipulation and firing of such a porcelain clay. I also think this clay is generously suited to the clean-burning, controllable electric atmosphere. Colour has always played a leading role in the 'feel' of the type of tableware I wanted to produce, and I thought that in making the switch to the electric kiln the way in which I was to apply the metal oxides and coloured stains should be a method in which I was already competent. As I had worked extensively with slips before it seemed a good idea to concentrate on using these, and slip decoration under a transparent glaze was the technique I adopted for my porcelain.

I have always greatly admired the honesty, strength and directness shown in the form and decoration of what is loosely termed 'peasant pottery,' from many periods and cultures. However, my own background and influences were very different from those of country potters – they belonged to the social order and economic pressures which accompany life in a large city. I was surrounded by junk and antique shops, house clearance sales and the flotsam of an ever-changing population: I saw pieces of Victoriana, Art Nouveau and Art Deco piled high on market stalls and in the houses of family and friends. On the whole much of this work sadly fails to realise an aesthetic balance, but some pieces have beautiful elements, qualities of form, line and colour which can be developed in modern studio ceramics. I also greatly admire the work produced by the Japanese Oribe potters of the Momoyama period, particularly the green Oribe pots. The work produced by the potters of the Nabeshima clan (where the designs are exclusive to the area of Arita) holds a fascination for me, and influences the work I produce now. Asymmetrical surface design was important in these two periods of Japanese ceramics, and I have developed my own particular techniques to try and assimilate that 'feel' in my work.

Porcelain dish, 18 inches wide. Clay additions to rim. Poured and trailed slip with underglaze colours sponge-stamped over the surface.

1 Using a plastic fork the clay can be marked in a swirling, lively, random fashion, giving the first layer of visual texture.

I begin the decoration of my pottery at the earliest stage possible, just after the piece has been thrown. Using fingers and some simple tools the pot can be manipulated and altered into a variety of different shapes. To provide texture and visual depth, I build up different layers throughout the decoration of the pot. At this stage, I use a plastic three-pronged fork to mark the clay in swirling, free and random patterns. These marks which initially look quite bold will give a subtle vitality to the clay body when fired. The plastic fork marks give the impression of floating under the surface of the subsequent layers of texturing. The sgraffito lines carved into the clay are done with no formal patterning in mind – I aim to create a feeling of vibrant energy and motion across the whole surface of the pot.

Using florist's wrapping paper, which has a good wet strength, I mask out areas on the surface of leatherhard pots; slip is then applied and when the paper mask or stencil is removed, the surface colour of the clay will be revealed. This method gives me two opposing areas, one of colour from the slip and the natural white of the porcelain clay. The blank flat whiteness gives me another space in which to develop my decoration.

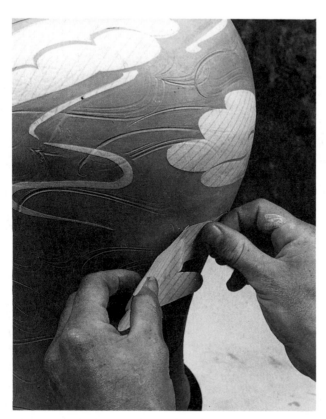

2 Cut paper shapes are used as a mask or stencil by being moistened and pressed firmly onto the pot. This method of resist will give a clearly defined, sharp edge to the blocked-out forms.

3 Liquid clay (slip) is poured onto the pot when in the leatherhard stage. The slip will be coloured by the addition of metal oxides.

4 Cut and shaped sponge stamps are employed to lift off the slip while still wet to reveal the clay body underneath.

5 The paper mask is lifted to give a broader space which can be decorated with a different method and concept.

When the pot is covered with liquid slip, large flat areas of colour are created which have little visual texture. To alter this, I use cut sponge stamps to take off, or lift the wet slip and reveal the white clay body underneath. I can also use the sponge stamps to apply colour to the pot.

These sponges can be made quite easily. First I draw a design in ink on the surface of a flat piece of manufactured foam (the grade can vary from close-knit to open texture, and the choice gives a different effect). Then, using a hot wire or needle, the pattern is burnt into the sponge. Many intricate and delicate designs can be produced by this method, and almost any pattern can be reproduced.

The motifs I use are most frequently floral – I apply these so that they seem to grow all over the work in random groupings, adding a lively yet subtle overall impression of texture and suggesting the profusion of growth found within nature. Occasionally I use a more precise symbol, not quite hidden within the mass of floral and leaf shapes – peering out, as if smothered by the surrounding greenery.

As a contrast to the random groups of sponge stamps, I take a more formal approach to the areas of white clay left after the paper mask has been removed. I use a variety of decorative methods, mainly slip trailing and brushwork, to create a more structured pattern on these areas, and aim to tie together the various elements already created over the surface of the pot. I believe this way of realising a decorative balance has similarities to the dyeing and painting techniques used by the makers of Japanese kimonos.

The two main surface areas, those of stamped, coloured slips and the slip trailed or painted white porcelain are set up in asymmetric opposition to each other, establishing an edge, a tension between the two forces – and this is integral to all my work.

By using different methods for decorating the contrasting surface areas, the effects achieved can be very diverse – but through the tensions and energies in the patterning, the overlapping of the imagery and the depth of texture and markings, I can achieve a sympathetic counterbalance which eventually produces a vibrant but harmonious object.

6 A slip trailer is used to pipe out the various coloured slips onto a previously defined area of the pot.

7 Brush decoration is overpainted in a stronger pigment, adding motion through the previously defined paper resisted shapes.

8 Floating floral motifs in polychromatic slips are laid down on the white background shapes. A more formal approach to patterning is sometimes employed within these previously masked out areas.

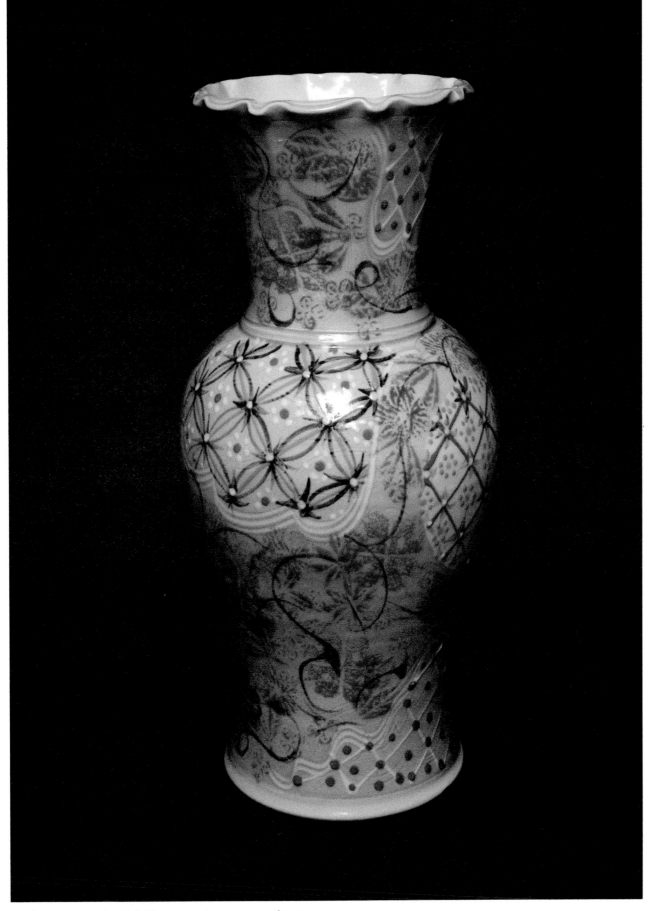

Porcelain vase, 22 inches high. The sponge stamps were used to stamp
colour onto the slip background. Brushwork and slip trailing employed.

Technical information

Slip

The four main slips I use are all based upon a white ball clay. This ball clay is processed by Watts Blake Bearne and is available under the code t.w.v.d. Using this clay as my base the following oxides are added to give the colours indicated.

Tan/pink
5% rutile

Green
2% copper carbonate
$\frac{1}{4}$% nickel oxide

Grey/blue
1% iron chromate
$\frac{1}{4}$% cobalt oxide

Dark grey
3% iron chromate
$\frac{1}{4}$% cobalt oxide

When mixing the brighter colours for slip trailing I use powdered porcelain clay (the same as the body) which forms a good white base to carry the various oxides and commercial stains. Although the t.w.v.d. ball clay itself fires white, present within it are certain impurities which will modify the bright qualities of bold colour, but add to the texture of the larger areas of poured slip. To the porcelain clay I add the following oxides and stains.

Yellow
10% yellow body stain (Potterycrafts p.4516)

Bright pink
15% coral red underglaze stain (Potterycrafts p.4481)

Violet
10% coral red underglaze stain
$\frac{1}{4}$% cobalt oxide

For the brushwork pigment I use the following.

Bright blue
92% powdered red earthenware clay
4% manganese oxide
4% cobalt oxide

Bright red
50% coral red underglaze stain
50% transparent glaze

Glaze is added to the stain for painting on the greenware to help fix it through sintering in the biscuit firing and forms a homogeneous fit in the final glaze firing.

When the pots are thoroughly dried I fire them over a period of approximately 18 hours to biscuit temperature (950°C). After cooling a transparent glaze is applied and the final firing temperature is achieved over 24 hours. The final temperature is determined by the maturing point of the glaze which in my case is approximately 1260°C (Orton cone 8).

This is the recipe of the glaze I use.

58% feldspar
16% whiting
6% china clay
15% flint
5% zinc oxide

To this formula I add 2% bentonite to aid suspension.

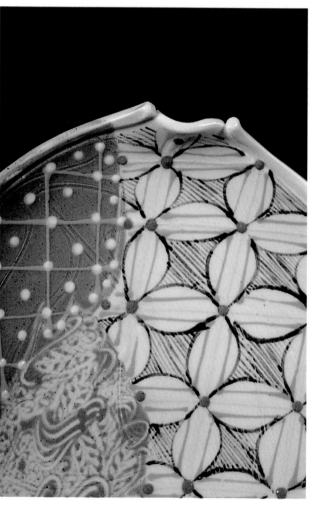

Detail of a square plate showing slip trailing, brushwork and sgraffito.

Photography by John Coles.

Porcelain teapot, slip decorated, cane handle. The slip has been lifted off by using cut sponge stamps, revealing the clay body underneath. The central motif masked out by a cut paper circle was slip trailed later.

John Maltby

Good at drawing at an early age, John gravitated naturally towards art school, where he decided that the sculpture department was the most interesting and chose to work there. More important, perhaps, was his discovery at the age of eighteen of a world of feeling outside the immediate material world. The main influence in this respect was music, particularly the work of Sibelius who, through his music conveyed the power of his feeling for nature and his country, Finland. Sibelius' life and work had a profound effect on John's thinking.

After leaving college, John taught art to school children and older students. During this period he read Bernard Leach's *A Potters' Book*: the first chapter expressed the view that pottery could be both aesthetically pleasing and functional, and that it could also be affordable. John found this view exciting and stimulating. He felt himself drawn away from sculpture towards an activity that could more easily bridge the gap between artist and public.

Fired with the enthusiasm to learn the skills necessary to become a potter, John sought the advice of Bernard Leach and eventually learnt his craft from working with David Leach. Because his primary objective was to explore the imagination and the relationships between the materials of expression and the thing to be expressed, John had to strike out on his own. He made domestic ware at first until he was firmly established but progressively each piece made became more individual in expression, and John began to see himself as an artist rather than a craftsman.

'Pottery at this stage in the twentieth century is in a unique position in that we can apply ourselves both to the functional and to the aesthetic sides of ceramics. As an artist I choose to develop the aesthetic side, drawing from those areas around me that artists have always drawn from, primarily the English land and seascape. One of the beauties of ceramics is that it has built into its nature the element of development in series, and that is what appeals to me. The refinement of an image over a rather quickly made series of pots, to arrive at a satisfactory conclusion which may start off in a tentative way, that is one of the greatest attractions of pottery for me, apart from the fact that it also deals with colour *and* form and is therefore perfectly capable of expressing whatever anyone wants to express.'

John controls the development of his design, consciously aware of the image he wants. But the feel and impact of the finished pot will be strongly affected by the way that the decoration is applied: a slip trailer, for example, makes a different mark from that made by a resist technique or by a brush. The choice of medium and method of application are therefore of the utmost importance.

'If you work with the natural nature of the material which you are using, you will tend to create beautiful marks rather than ugly marks. The things that I like the most are closest to the medium they were made from; these are the most beautiful, whether they be Cycladic figures, Henry Moore's sculpture or the paintings of Alfred Wallis which I am particularly fond of.'

John's method of applying colour and pattern to the surface of his pots is an integral part of a progression of ideas and techniques which starts in the forming process. He builds up images simply and directly; forms reflect the decoration and decoration reflects the form and equal consideration is given to weight of form, motifs, and the subtlety of surface. John synthesises these elements together into a cohesive whole. This integrated way of making pots inevitably reflects his mood whether that be volatile or sombre, colourful or drab. The apparent simplicity of his art is achieved through a thorough knowledge of pottery making and techniques. Although the controlled relationship between form and colour is important to John, he also appreciates the vitality of imperfections and is not interested in craftsmanship for craftsmanship's sake.

'Craftsmanship for me means finding the freedom through understanding the materials which then allows one to give energy to the more important, immediate, drama of the object; but if craftsmanship is seen as a way of parading one's cleverness, then I want nothing of it.'

John's strong connection to his subject and medium begins in the very first stages of pot making. He uses a mixture of three basic materials for his clay: white ball clay, molochite and plastic craft crank clay (from Potclays). The subtleties of clay colour are not important to John but the clay has to feel right for the type of piece to be made. For instance, throwing clay would consist of three parts white ball clay and one part molochite; clay for hand-building would be craft crank which is much coarser; and extruding clay would be ball clay and craft crank in a fifty/fifty mix with the addition of molochite.

Materials are mixed by hand from powder to plastic without soaking, then moulded into manageable lumps which are wrapped in polythene to age and to form a homogeneous mass. Kneading the clay acts as a period of reflection when John's imagination is stimulated and a plan of procedure suggested whereby he can give form to his ideas.

2 Above: All components for the finished piece are made at the same time. After trimming the sides are put on one side until the base is decorated.

3 Below: Soft clay is pushed and spread across the surface of the clay slab.

1 Slices are cut from a large block of grogged clay.

'Black Flowers', stoneware bottle, 10 inches × 10 inches. Glaze resist with black, red and blue enamels.

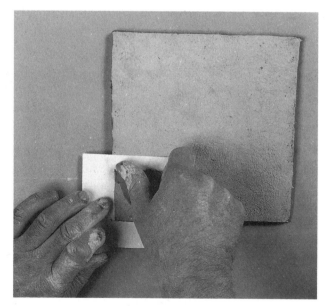

4 Different coloured clays are pushed through a card stencil, building up a chequer board of coloured squares.

John's production is split between hand-building and throwing, with approximately seventy per cent hand-built pieces to thirty per cent thrown pots. Forms consist mainly of footed bowls, jugs, some teapots, dishes and covered pots.

Because he enjoys the asymmetry of nature, John tends to alter any symmetry created through the throwing process. His bowls for example, are altered whilst on the wheel. A large soft extruded slab of clay may be attached to the rim to add visual weight and presence. This is something that he equates with the massive quality found in Gothic architecture. (Wells cathedral in Somerset is a constant source of inspiration for both form and decoration and John often revisits it.)

Because form and decoration are of equal importance John has developed a swift and rhythmic flow of production which applies whether the piece be thrown or hand-built. Slab dishes are made in the same rhythm as the thrown bowls.

John is totally involved in the flow of his work and this intensity of working produces some interesting accidental results. He may use the palm of his hand to soften and thin the edge of a pot, thus creating a gentle rhythm of slight undulations. But there may be an interruption of his flow, resulting in too great or too little pressure of the palm — and a discordant break in the line of the rim follows. John looks at this discordant note in the flow of the rim and decides how to deal with it. Often he makes a feature of this break in the rhythm by cutting out that part of the rim to form a new shape. He sets out to develop such accidents and to allow himself to be stimulated by them.

John works at such speed that he can at no time consider a piece of work as a formulation of separate components — it holds together as one. As the parts of, say, a dish, are all at the same stage of plasticity no compound is needed in the form of slurry to bond the pieces together, and this allows him an uninterrupted flow of making. John has been able to develop his own method of applying coloured slips, the texture and stiffness of the decorating clay being of prime importance. It must not be too sticky nor too stiff, and it must be able to move and flow when pushed across the surface of the base clay. The right consistency is helped by the addition of fairly coarse molochite (30's to dust). Because none of the decorating clay is in liquid form, all layers of decoration can be applied at almost the same stage.

Decorating clay is made from soft white clay to which commercial stains and oxides are added for colouring. The choice of colour reflects his moods. Sober shades of green, brown, grey, etc. may recall the coastal areas of Lincolnshire (where John spent his childhood) on a cold

November day, or the sombrely soaring, massive architecture of Wells cathedral. Blues, fiery oranges, yellow and reds can all lend a vibrancy and feeling of light to a piece inspired by the English summer landscape.

John often uses card stencils through which he applies the coloured clay and those surfaces are then brushed with pigment or patterned with sgraffito or stamping. John never feels inhibited in his choice of decorating tool – he will use whatever the piece seems to require, from the wrong end of a brush to his thumbprint. This is also true when decoration is carried out at some other stage, such as glazing or enamelling after the first glaze firing.

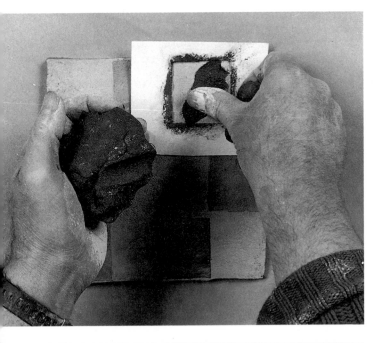

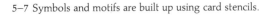
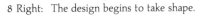

5–7 Symbols and motifs are built up using card stencils.

8 Right: The design begins to take shape.

John's expressive capacity is noticeable in the way that he applies decoration. Slow or vigorous, with grave care or lively abandonment, each gesture of application indicates a bond between an experience and how that experience emerges in a finished motif. A stormy day may provoke the need to apply colour in a vigorous manner that will convey something of the bright cloud-scudding sky; however, as John points out:

'It is very difficult when making a mark on clay to *choose* a motif, because the motif tends to be something recollected in tranquillity and the gesture of mark making is something done spontaneously. That is a dilemma one has to resolve in one's work.'

9 Smaller motifs are used to tie in the various elements.

10 The finished soft clay design is ready for the sides to be attached. A sketch of the design is shown here.

Pots are made in small runs of fifteen to twenty and ideas flow from evaluating these runs. John feels that his confidence in the decorative images develops the more he works on each run. These groups of pots are usually decorated to express two themes, a visit to Wells cathedral or a seaport, for example. John likes to imagine a piece in a setting: for example, a jug form may be visualised in the deep-set recess of a Cornish cottage window or a dish in the context of a modern room. This helps to establish the mood of the work.

Although John limits the number of forms that he chooses to make, his forms are all intimately connected, fitting neatly into the human scale of things. He wants to create a certain sense of intimacy between the maker and the user. Large-scale work, on the other hand, can be intimidating and aggressive.

John assimilates and uses many images for his decoration: flowers from a country garden, fish which become nets and nets which become rocks and buoys, houses, estuaries, lily leaves and a leaping tiger seen on the wall of Wells cathedral. All these things can be seen in the robust, direct and sensitive work he creates, influenced as he is by the English tradition of painting landscape and sea.

It is my opinion that John Maltby is one of this century's most significant artists in clay, and that his work has an enduring and timeless quality, portraying deep emotions through a simple direct approach to the use of technique and materials.

Technical information

White slip
50% molochite
50% ball clay h.v.a.r.

Coloured clay
120 grams white plastic clay, coloured with varied amounts of stains, oxides, etc. These are kneaded in with a little water; this way small amounts of many colours can be produced quickly.

black
100% white clay
10% black stain (medcol/1713)

grey
50% white clay
50% black clay

green
100% white clay
5% chrome oxide

dark blue
100% white clay
2% cobalt oxide
1% iron oxide

Coloured decorating glaze
Varying percentages of commercial stain are added to simple clear glaze. Direct painting pigments are produced by adding 2 parts glaze to one part of pigment (stain or oxide). From the maturing temperature of the glaze (approximately 1285°C) the kiln is cooled rapidly to 1000°C to stop the recrystallisation of the glaze.

Photography by John Coles.

11 The sides of the dish are joined to the base.

'Landscape with Gothic Flowers', irregular pressed dish, 12 inches × 10 inches. Stoneware, painted slips with red and blue enamels. (The enamels are applied and fired in a third firing at 775°C.)

'Flowers in a Landscape', large jugs, 14 inches high. Stoneware, resisted glazes.

Dorothy Feibleman

Dorothy Feibleman grew up in mid-western America, in an area surrounded by woods and cornfields. Dorothy's mother and aunt, who had both studied painting, took their children to many activities held at the local Art Museum, and the Indianapolis Children's Museum. Dorothy spent almost every Saturday at the Children's Museum, where she became absorbed in crafts, ethnography and natural history. Her grandfather's collection of artefacts, excavated during his travels in South America, was also a source of wonderment.

Dorothy's involvement with the Children's Museum increased when they sponsored her to collect information, photographs and objects for an east European gallery. Since this time she has continued to photograph the craft processes, tools and the finished objects in use in traditional village life in eastern Europe.

'What I find interesting in many of the villages I have visited is that everyone has acquired a wide range of skills. Most villagers think three-dimensionally. Unlike highly industrialised people, whose possessions are mostly 'store-bought', peasants can sense quality in workmanship and materials because they produce most of their own possessions themselves. They have to know these things to survive. I find the people easy to communicate with, because through my work I have acquired the same thought processes. I feel that watching other people make things, seeing their tools and watching their processes, as well as absorbing many other intangible elements, can be related to and used directly in my own work.'

This fundamental attitude to raw materials and her intimate knowledge of the quality of these materials have had a profound influence on the way in which Dorothy approaches and executes her own work.

While at Rochester Institute of Technology Dorothy became interested in lamination techniques, as a result of making laminated beads and pots. (Lamination means the fusing together of sheets of any material.) From working with clay, she began to investigate the structural nature of lamination and how the techniques are used within a number of crafts. She wrote a thesis on the subject in 1972–73.

'It is important to see and understand the techniques used in other crafts. They can be transferred and adapted. Any material can be laminated. It always amazes me that every day I come into contact with so many laminated objects.'

Based in England since 1973, Dorothy has used her knowledge of lamination in many of the forms and patterns that she creates today in clay. This article will concentrate on her work in lamination, although she is equally well-known for her inlay and pierced work.

A selection of porcelain and gold jewellery.
(Photo: Christie's Colour Library)

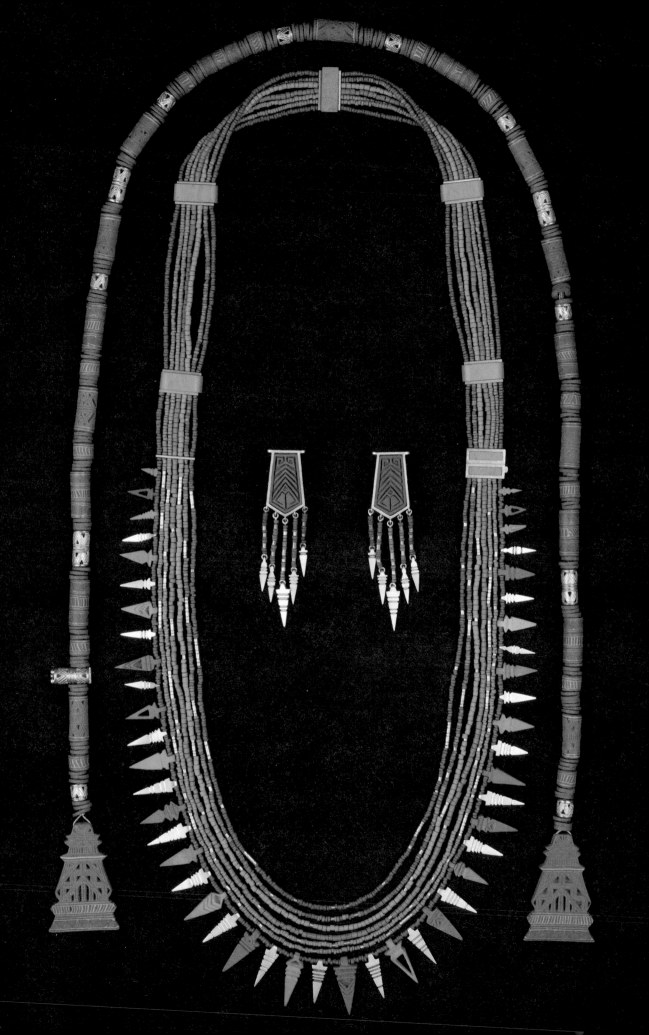

Dorothy looks towards processes and techniques practised by crafts people in other disciplines to inspire new working methods and ways of adapting her own work. Often she works with other people, combining skills from separate disciplines in joint projects. She learns as much as she can of the other skills during the process. As a result of soaking up a diversity of techniques, Dorothy has developed her own tools and jigs. Her open-minded attitude towards technique allows her to see and employ elements of her lamination methods in many of the other things she does.

'I often relate food to the way I make pots. Making shushi or a layered torte can exemplify the similarities shared by all mediums.'

A technique, a form, a pattern or a combination of colours may all be the beginning of Dorothy's working periods. Whichever initial spark starts the process, other considerations can stimulate the way in which a piece will finally emerge – differences in the lamination and in the ways of cutting and combining are only decided when work is in progress. Her continual experiments with method, colour, pattern and form ensures a healthy and lively approach to structuring her work, constantly providing new interest and individuality.

'The most exciting thing for me in using lamination in clay is that the structure and decoration are integral. The colourants, clay patterns and temperature you fire to all have a bearing on the form.'

The smooth making operation relies on thorough preparation of both raw materials and tools. Dorothy usually makes a large quantity of powdered white clay which she divides into quantities of approximately 25 lb batches that she colours with oxides and stains. Coloured stains are sometimes ball milled before mixing with the clay as they can then be more thoroughly mixed. Dorothy is always investigating the possibility of using new colours, from many sources, and makes test pieces to determine the potential of these colours and the quantities of stain and oxide to be added to a batch of clay.

Often she halves, quarters or even doubles the manufacturer's recommended quantity to see what effects and quality can be achieved in the finished result. Overloading with, say, copper oxide produces a certain volatile effect in clay which contrasts with the layer of more stable clay next to it. This attitude of investigation and experiment allows Dorothy a fuller range of expression in the structure and patterning of her pots. Similarly, she is not restricted to any one type of clay nor to any one firing temperature: she uses clays which range from relatively low-firing Parian to high-firing porcelains.

The batches of coloured clays are mixed with water and blunged into a slip consistency before being pushed through a vibratory sieve to form a smooth creamy slip. The slip is dried out to a workable plastic consistency on cloth covered plaster bats before being passed through a pugmill and stored in polythene. This method ensures even colour distribution throughout the batch of clay.

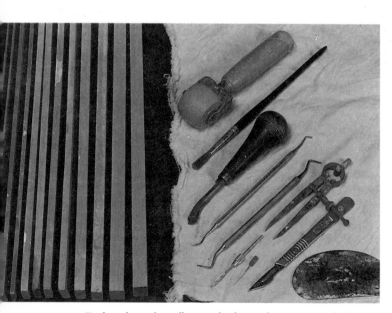

1 Tools and wooden rolling guides for producing various thicknesses of clay sheets.

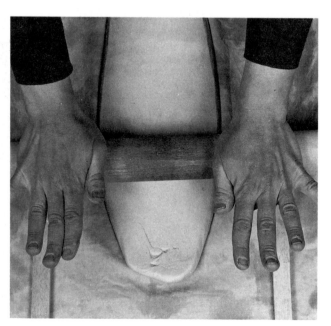

2 Rolling clay to set thickness.

The making of one style of pot is described below and illustrated in the accompanying photos.

Before beginning a piece of work Dorothy assembles the clays and tools that she will need, and decides on the heights of the wooden rolling guide to use for the thicknesses of the clay sheets that she requires. Using the appropriate wooden guide, she rolls out a variety of thicknesses on linen backcloths (using a different cloth for each colour). She produces clay sheets of differing thickness and contrasting colour. Alternatively, she could produce sheets of contrasting colour but of the same thickness. These sheets are trimmed and slipped and then laid on top of each other, in pairs of the same thickness.

Dorothy then uses a rolling guide on its side as a straight-edge (the height of it acts as a thickness guide) and cuts slices from the paired sheets of clay. These slices have the stripes of colour running lengthwise. These slices are then slipped (slip can be of different colours) and combined together by compressing them between the rolling guides on a linen backcloth to form a sheet of striped clay. The

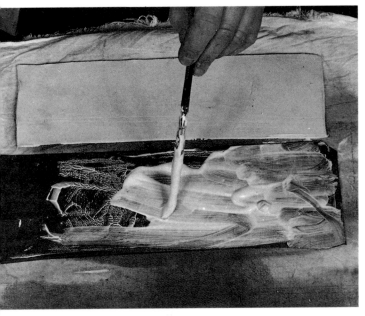

3 Slipping the clay sheets.

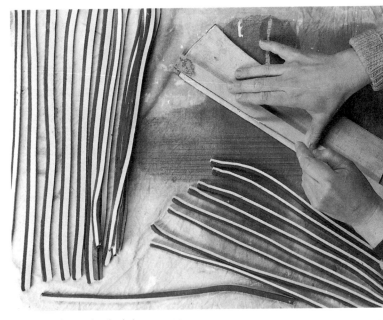

5 Cutting the sandwiched clay into strips.

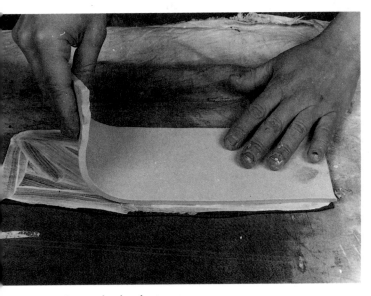

4 Joining the clay sheets.

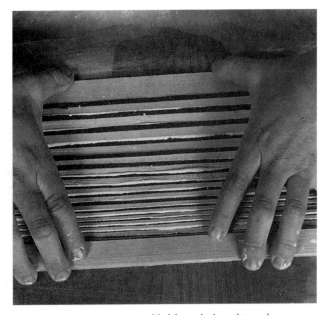

6 The slipped strips are reassembled from thick to thin and compressed between the rolling guides.

thickness of the bands of colour gradually decreases as each slice is added. When Dorothy decides that the slab contains the right number of slices, she scrapes off any excess slip with a metal kidney. She then picks up the slab by its backcloth and turns it over so that she may scrape off excess slip from this side, also.

Dorothy may employ a wedge-shape template to cut further slices from the new slab. The wedge-shape slices (with stripes running crosswise) are placed aside until it is time to assemble them. Dorothy then rolls out a thin slab of

7 The sheet of stripped clay is cleaned by scraping (the clay is reversed by turning it over on the linen backcloth and cleaning is repeated).

9 Wedge shape strips ready for reassembly.

8 A cardboard template is used to cut wedge shape lengths.

10/11 Each strip is given a thin edging of clay.

clay as a base and coats it with slip. She then lays each wedge-shape slice on its edge on this base and cuts out through it, leaving a layer of the thin slab clay on the edge of each slice. The wedge-shape slices are then slipped on the slab clay edge, then appropriately curved and joined to the next one to produce a spiralled shape on a fresh tightly woven cotton backcloth. When Dorothy has completed the spiral pattern, she again scrapes off any excess slip and presses a clean linen cloth over the shape, which she lifts and turns over before scraping off excess slip from the other surface.

The two inner edges of the spiral shape are slipped so that they may be joined. Dorothy lifts the spiral and brings together the two slipped edges to form a rudimentary cone. The cone is then eased into a biscuit fired mould where it stiffens overnight.

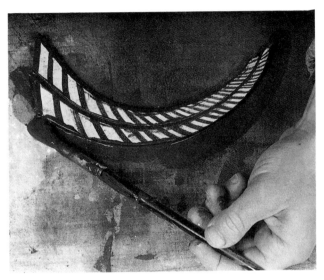

12 The wedge shape strips are slipped and attached to each other to form a spiral.

14 The two inner edges are slipped.

13 The spiralled slab of clay is scraped clean, reversed, and cleaned on the back again.

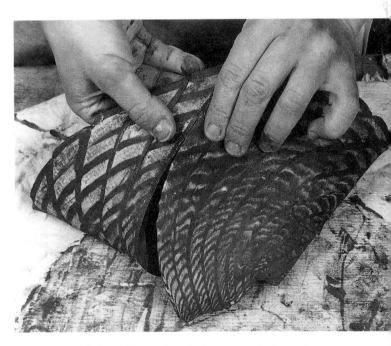

15 The slab is lifted and the two slipped edges are attached to each other to create a rudimentary cone form.

When Dorothy judges that the cone has stiffened up enough to be satisfactorily handled, she turns it out of the mould and reverses it back onto a wheel where she closes the open point of the cone to form the base for the bowl that is being made. The cone is then dropped into the biscuit-fired mould. Dorothy uses a small roller to compress and consolidate the clay against the inner surface of the mould and levels the top edge with the same roller. She cuts a measured strip of clay in a chosen colour and attaches it with slip to the top edge to form a rim. She scrapes and cleans the inside of the bowl to reveal the spiralling pattern of laminated coloured clays. Dorothy waits for the bowl to be dry enough to drop cleanly from the mould before scraping and cleaning the outside, again to reveal the patterning. She then wraps the bowl in thin polythene (usually dry cleaning bags) and returns it to the mould to dry out slowly and completely. When the clay is bone dry, Dorothy works on the surface to clean it

16 The cone is dropped into a biscuit fired mould and allowed to stiffen.

18 The pot is returned to the mould and consolidated with a small roller.

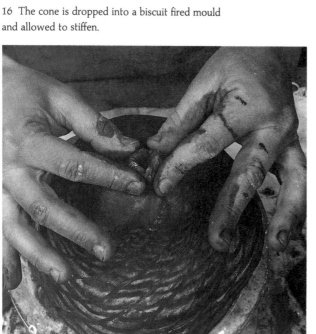

17 When stiff enough to handle the piece is dropped out of the mould, placed on a wheel and the base 'thrown' closed.

19 The top is rolled flat.

thoroughly and to remove any smudges on the colourful and patterned surface.

Dorothy decides the firing according to the clay used, the form itself (some forms need support in the kiln) and whether any glaze is to be used. This decision may well not be made until the making process is complete, for Dorothy may have changed or added to the construction and pattern first intended.

Although Dorothy does not consciously use historical references when formulating her patterns, she feels that some patterns are subconsciously universal, and that making processes with some local variations may also be universal. Dorothy's sense of craftsmanship demands close attention to minute detail in the making and finishing – this is displayed quite dramatically in the intricately detailed laminated and carved jewellery that she also produces.

Although other people are using lamination within their work, Dorothy Feibleman is concentrating on exploring the full potential of this form of decoration. By her open-minded approach to all aspects of her work, two-dimensional and three-dimensional, and by immersing herself in all the possibilities of the lamination technique, Dorothy is not only producing exciting and individual pieces of jewellery and pots but is also developing new ways of structuring and patterning laminated clay.

20 A strip of clay is cut from a small rolled-out slab.

22 Both the inside and outside of the pot are scraped clean.

21 The strip is attached to the rim.

23 The pot is wrapped in polythene and allowed to dry out slowly.

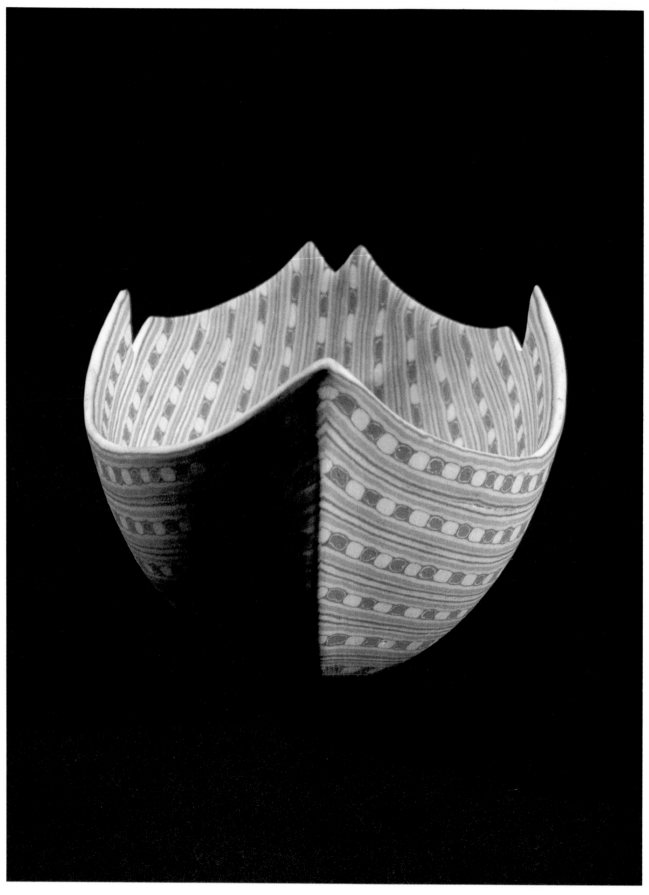

Technical information

'I mostly use commercial stains, but I also use oxides. Different textures can be obtained from using either different types of clay bodies, such as porcelain or parian fired to porcelain temperatures, which create shiny and matt variations; overloading a clay body with vanadium, copper oxide or a lead based frit which with porcelain or parian create tiny, even air bubbles under the surface and give a raised texture. I prefer to mix my clay by weighing it out in dry form and adding dry colourants so I get repeatable results. When I test, as a rule, I try 20% colourants down to 0.5% colourants. This way I have a treasure trove to delve into.

If you don't want to experiment with your own clay bodies, these ideas can be applied to any commercial clays. If you want to mix colourants with plastic clay, it is best to slake a set amount of clay and combine measured-out and watered-down stain or oxide with the slip, and then wedge it into a quantity of plastic clay.'

Photography by John Coles.

Opposite: 'Asymmetrical Bowl', $3\frac{3}{4}$ inches long, 3 inch diameter and $2\frac{1}{2}$ inches tall. Laminated porcelain, polished after each firing, with silicon carbide paper.

'Lunar Bowl', 5 inches wide, 3 inches high. Porcelain, the dark areas from overloaded copper oxide, the white edges overloaded with a frit.

Dorothy Hafner

In the course of the last ten years of pottery making Dorothy Hafner's artistic and professional directions have changed frequently, but through all the changes there has been a constant interest in making things in series, of employing pattern, colour and decoration in both the structure and the surface of objects, and in making things that are functional.

'In the early to mid 1970s when I began my career just out of college, designing and producing functional objects was not a very popular pursuit amongst American ceramicists. Two attitudes prevailed at the time. One was that in order to make crafts appreciated as art the maker was wise to create objects that looked more like art, and less like pottery. The other was that works produced in multiples were more commercial and not as serious as those created only once.

Today, in the mid 1980s things are much different. There is a healthier response to functional object making. Increasing numbers of not only potters but architects and sculptors are creating functional tablewares with the same seriousness with which they create their other works. Where one might refer to the 1960s as the height of the craft movement, the 1980s are perhaps the time of a new design renaissance.'

Though Dorothy's formal training was in fine art and studio pottery, she has in the last ten years acquired the various industrial skills required both to produce her work independently with a small staff or to license designs to industry. These include mechanical drawing skills, plaster carving, mould and model making, artwork preparation for decal decoration and, most importantly, selling an idea to a client.

Her first retail clients for her own hand-painted dinnerwares were Tiffany's and Neiman Marcus; to work with them she presented glazed prototypes of the actual objects. For the last four years she has also been working with The Rosenthal Studio-Linie in West Germany under a licensing contract. Her designs are presented to this firm as drawings or plaster models but in many cases she prefers to present a glazed ceramic prototype as she still feels most comfortable realising her ideas three-dimensionally in clay.

At present Dorothy has a staff of five in her New York City studio—a slip caster, two painters, an office manager and a studio manager. They spend most of their time producing pieces from her eight studio dinnerware collections but also assist her in other projects such as tile commissions, prototype development for new products, research, and one of a kind object making which she continues to do.

To create her work Dorothy begins with an idea – from there, the methods of developing that idea vary widely and in some cases she may draw and sketch for weeks. In others she may work directly in clay, manipulating clay loosely to achieve a certain shape or profile. In other cases she works in paper, cutting and folding shapes to see how they look – Dorothy likes paper because it is quick, neat, and easy to store.

Opposite: 'Mardi Gras Ribbons', porcelain platter, 17 inches each side, 1983.

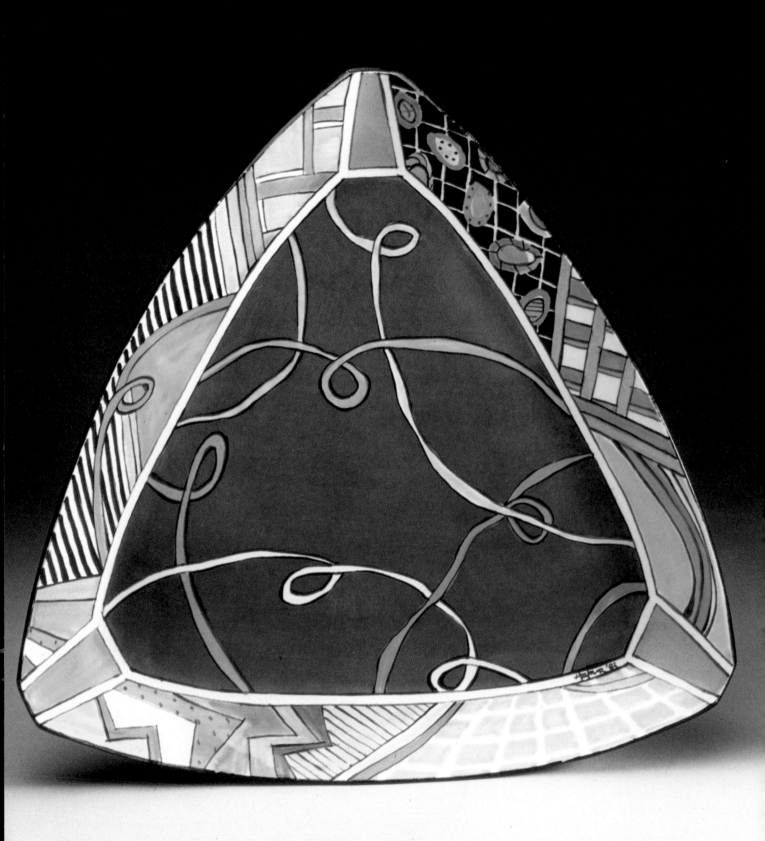

'Kyoto Homage', porcelain tea service, 1980.

'My ideas and inspirations are as varied as my methods. Much of my early work was drawn directly from the urban landscape and so was very geometrical and colourful. Later, I became more interested in outer-space images and technologies and juxtaposing them with motifs and images from primitive cultures.

Every time I travel I get inspired. After a week lying under palm trees in the sun I find myself using stylised floral or aquatic motifs. After a trip to the American west I find myself using a mesa or canyon profile as a motif. If I listen to African music my marks are bold and colourful, if I listen to Frank Sinatra my marks are lighter, looser and more lyrical. It is safe to say, then, that the art I am making at any given time is a response to what I am seeing, hearing or smelling at that time.'

The ceramic process is lengthy – as weeks lapse between the different stages it is easy to forget the original idea that inspired the work, and to maintain a consistency of thought or mood throughout the development of a particular piece or collection. Dorothy often uses music as a device, listening to the same tape, artist, or style of music throughout a whole project, particularly if she is having trouble getting into the right mood after having been away from the project for a while.

In her early work from 1975–1980 Dorothy was mainly involved in developing surface decoration. In keeping with this she purposely designed shapes which were clean, simple and geometric and wouldn't compete with her decoration. She made every effort to make them functional, easy to use, clean, and store, and in most cases, she was successful.

'By 1980, however, my decoration had become so aggressive that it was just about bursting off these shapes. At that point I decided to stop decorating my square shapes, in fact to stop decorating altogether. Instead, I decided to take a year or so and to concentrate on developing new shapes that could carry my new style of decoration. This meant that I wanted the new forms to have the same spirit about them as my decoration. My decoration had become much more aggressive and so my shapes should too. My decision was that if I were to use a lightning bolt motif or a chequerboard, why not cut the contour of the shape in the same way? Why not fashion my shapes the way I clothed them?'

The result was two new bodies of work. One was an ongoing series of soup tureens, punch bowls, pasta services and vases, all with cutaway tops and sides. The second was a triangular and trapezoidal dinner service which she later licensed to Rosenthal.

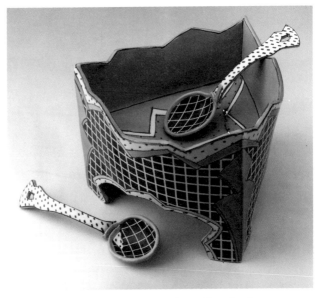

'Pasta Server with Two Spoons', porcelain with underglaze decoration, 1984.

'Lightning Bolt Punchbowl and Spoon', with underglaze decoration, 1984.

Above: 'Blue Loop with Head-dress', porcelain coffee and dessert service. Hand-painted underglaze decoration, 1984.

Dorothy Hafner painting a one of a kind platter. A flat board is rested on the platter from rim to rim. This serves to support the hand while painting straight lines over the curvilinear surface of the platter.

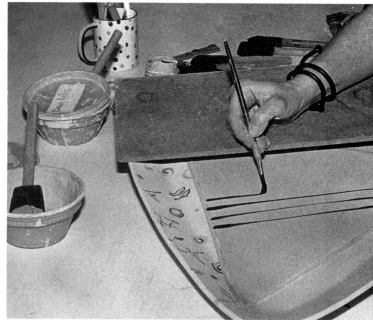

'Stats' dinner service, porcelain with underglaze decoration, 1984.
Hand-printed, 100% cotton napkins by The Fabric Workshop and Dorothy Hafner.

When she first began developing these shapes, Dorothy started by making an actual tracing of her earlier decorative patterns. From that tracing she created a template which would be used to cut a slab of clay which would be used to form the side of a new form. Later she abandoned this method and created profiles inspired by, but not copied from, her decoration. Dorothy still finds it useful to remember the exercise, as it reinforces one of the concepts that she works with, which is to create shapes to carry specific decoration, rather than shapes that can carry any decoration.

In decorating her work, both one of a kind pieces and production items, Dorothy tends to use a five colour system plus black. Though she occasionally creates simpler black and white pieces, she is most satisfied using lots of colours.

'When there are lots of colours and yet no one is dominant it is pleasing to my eye. Then, depending on my mood, or how I am setting my table or arranging my home, I can play up or down any of the five different colours that I choose. This flexibility is appealing to me as these are objects that I hope will be around for more than a season in someone's home.'

All of Dorothy's pieces are cone 7 porcelain. Each is decorated with coloured slips applied to the biscuited work (cone 06), and then sprayed with a thin coat of clear glaze before being high fired in an oxidising atmosphere. The methods she uses are fairly straightforward graphic techniques, a combination of hand painting with a brush, and stencilling. In stencilling she uses a variety of materials available through art suppliers or stationers to mask off areas before colour application, including masking tapes in all widths and gummed labels. They are pressed on the ware, painted over, and then removed. She also uses contact paper, cutting her own shapes as needed. In many cases she finds it as easy to hand paint the colour on as it is to cut elaborate stencils which can only be used once. For painting a full range of brush sizes are kept on hand.

'I was brought up watching lots of television so it is no surprise that there is a cartoon quality to much of my work. The bright colours and black outlining are very much a result of this experience.'

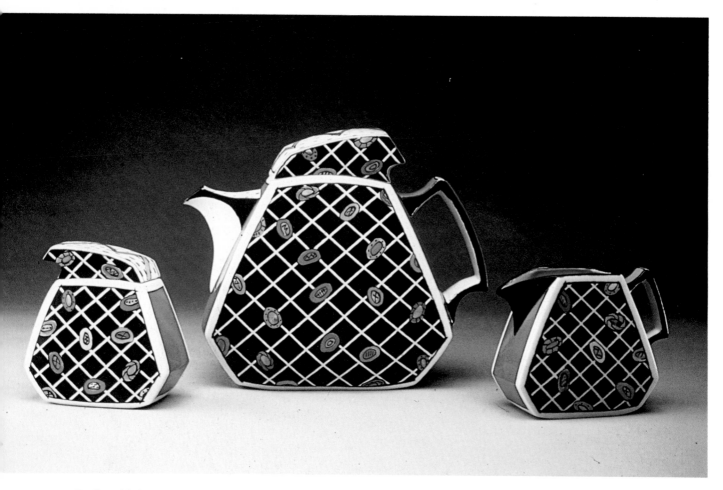

'Satellite', (black) porcelain teapot, sugar bowl and creamer, 1984.

Opposite: Three vases, 1984
'Mint Grid', 12$\frac{1}{2}$ inches high.
'Black Silhouette', 10$\frac{1}{2}$ inches high.
'Black Lattice', 14$\frac{1}{2}$ inches high.

All photographs by Stephanie Baker Vail.

Archie McCall

Archie McCall was born and brought up in Dumfries in Scotland. After failing to gain entry into art college on leaving school in 1969, he spotted an advertisement in a local newspaper for a potter's apprentice. His interest in pottery had at that time been aroused by an attraction towards Oriental philosophy, particularly Buddhism, and he had seen and appreciated Japanese tea bowls. He gained the post and worked for John Davey in Kirkcudbrightshire for three years, learning to make pots very much in the Leach manner.

At the end of the apprenticeship he felt it time to move on, and an opportunity arose to travel to Korea and Japan. It was a journey which deeply affected him in many different ways. Travelling out with the romantic notion of exploring the Far East, it came as a shock to witness the brutality of the political regime he encountered in Korea.

'I went to Korea naïvely, as a visitor, to look at pots and to search out something of a culture, and in the end came away disturbed by the overriding impression of injustice and suffering, so that although the trip to the Far East was supposed to establish my ceramic credentials begun during the apprenticeship it was not used in that way at all. For a long time after that I became very concerned about the relevance of what I was doing.'

After returning from the East Archie established his first workshop in Garlieston, in Wigtownshire. From there he returned to Dumfries to be resident potter at Gracefield Arts Centre. This lasted from 1975 to 1978, when a gradual dissatisfaction with the structure and content of the ware he was producing coupled with an increasing interest in two-dimensional work led to his decision to study painting and ceramics at Edinburgh College of Art. He often painted from the landscape during this period, and he feels that his current ceramic decoration always returns to his Scottish environment. It is both the constancy and variety of landscape which appeals to him, and the fact that these are experiences which are shared by everyone, in both town and countryside. And this awareness of universal acceptance is also important in his response to other artists:

'The potters I admire, Hamada, or John Maltby, or the Oribe ware, for example, and also painters such as Klee, Morandi, Alan Davie, Julius Bissier, all tend to work within precise guidelines, they choose a particular scale or mode of operation and this, I found, gradually interested me in what I call 'small art' as opposed to grand gallery statements, whether it be in painting or in the applied arts. I do not consider this phrase derogatory, it often implies good humour and sensitivity and an optimism (which may be spiritual) within the establishment of a visual order. If anything my work has moved towards this smaller domestic level, it has to maintain some kind of human scale. If it becomes too far removed from people then I do not think it is fulfilling its function.'

After developing a strong two-dimensional discipline through painting Archie returned to pottery and its tra-

ditions. Combining his skills as a potter and his eye as a painter Archie's work has elements of lively good humour – he plays little tricks with himself which are contained within the pieces he makes. Often he structures his pots asymmetrically, to challenge himself when balancing the decoration. These are hidden areas of his work which are a pleasure to discover.

'I look for goodly humour in my pots, ideally it would be nice if people came away from my work smiling. Although I am not a practising Buddhist I still feel close to its philosophy and I think this aspect of humour is important in many Oriental religions and attitudes.'

Archie is not interested in making pots purely as products for a consumer – if this alone were in the forefront of his thinking then the work would become sterile for him.

Three press-moulded dishes
Bottom left: rectangular dish, glazed in white, blue and copper red. Latex resist motifs in black and green. Brushwork in green, black and blue. $13 \times 9\frac{3}{4}$ inches.

Top: square dish, glazed blue and white. Brushwork in green, black and gold, with low temperature red. 11 inch diameter.

Bottom right: square dish, glazed in white, black, blue and copper red. Latex resist in black and white. Brushwork in black, blue and green. 11 inch diameter.

He views each piece that he makes as a separate statement of values and each pot poses different decorative possibilities and different aesthetic problems. His forms tend to be constructed with surface pattern in mind; pieces with large smooth surfaces dominate his production, and he realises that the more complex shapes are not always the most successful when decorated.

He uses a white stoneware clay based upon ball clay and china clay (grolleg) which offers a white, smooth background to carry the decoration. Archie uses a number of forming methods for his plates and dishes: some are thrown using a Leach kickwheel for its slow, rhythmic qualities, and others are press moulded over hump moulds which emphasise the inside surface of the pot. Other hand-built dishes have flat rolled clay bases with extruded edges attached, diverse shapes to be made from these sections. Edges may also be cut, and by doing this any warpage arising from the joining of hand-formed elements and alignment of clay particles in the flat slabs used for press moulding can be physically and optically minimised. For instance, if the edge of a dish diverts from a straight edge because small pieces have been cut out, any movement of the form during firing will be less noticeable. Also by manipulating the edges of hand-built dishes the stresses set up

1 Above: Glaze is poured and then overpoured on the surface of the dish.

2 Below: Liquid latex is brushed onto the glaze to resist and define an area.

3 Right: The area is painted with contrasting dark pigment.

during construction can be dissipated. Archie takes the decoration into account here and may use the edge as a focus for his surface motifs.

Archie spends a long time constructing his pots before biscuit firing them, and then decorates a batch of work intensely, concentrating on the images and the energy of mark making. He begins by laying down a background of either a white or a celadon glaze. The basis of these glazes is cornish stone, which because of its hard, dry quality in the raw state helps the flow of brushed coloured glazes over the surface as it doesn't become too powdery while drying. Archie can glaze a batch of work in the morning knowing that all day remains for decorating. He uses simple stained glazes, adding oxides, stains, underglaze colour stains or any other compatible pigments by eye to the base glaze, and applies them to the pots by a variety of methods.

Although the decoration may seem simple it has a complex evolution. Both his earlier painting and pottery had a literal, representational quality, since when his essential subject matter has been expressed increasingly through evocative abstract imagery.

'Working on top of a damp, base glaze allows such layering of glaze or oxide as is necessary to build up a depth of surface; it also requires immediate decisions to be taken which, at the best of times, can allow intuition to take over from the intellect. When I decorate I make the first mark and each further mark is made in relation to the previous one. I am constantly looking to see how they relate to the form, weight and line of the pot.'

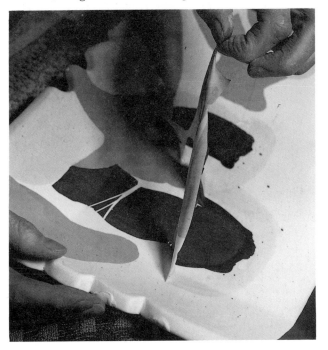

The quality of the marks and the method of making them is clearly very important. Pouring, dipping and painting are the chief ways that Archie applies glaze to the base glaze. Poured colour can lend a loose quality to a tight form, or act as a counter to a dipped or masked-out straight edge. Quality of line is also important; with his painter's sensibility, Archie is conscious of the infinite possibilities of a simple brushed line as it moves across the surface of the work. Sometimes he uses liquid latex to mask out areas on the glazed surface, and the slightly powdery quality of the glaze allows the latex to be released easily. Often the latex produces a hard edge to the motif which he can use to advantage – if a softer line is needed he will scratch through one glaze revealing the colour underneath, and Archie plays off these qualities of soft/hard, dark/light, straight/curved, one against another.

'To use a soft poured mark against a harder edge or latexed area is a combination which generally works for me. When I feel insecure in what I am doing the marks become pretty and when I feel confident the marks become less so, more direct, and I take risks; this is a see-saw I can see myself being on for a long time, in varying degrees.'

4 Left: The latex is removed.

5 Right: Fine free-flowing lines are painted to define another area.

6–8 Elements of the design are gradually brought together by using brushwork and dots of colour.

9 Opposite: The decorated dishes before firing.

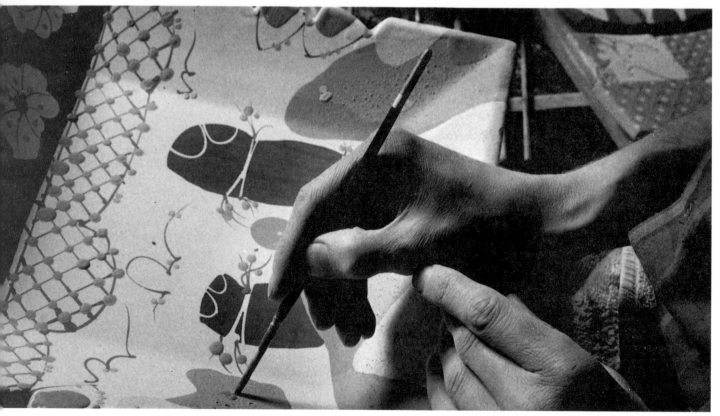

After glazing the pieces are fired in a reduction atmosphere to the maturing temperature of the clay and glazes, around 1280°C. For Archie to open the kiln and see exactly what was expected when he glazed the pots is to some extent a disappointment – for him, occasional accidents can spark off new ideas and directions. Overfiring, for instance, can allow the glaze to flow, softening a previously tightly painted image; equally, new colours and combinations can occur during the firing – for instance, a soft, spreading, rutile-based dot of colour which emerges from the firing with fuzzy edges could be used next time deliberately over a strict and rigid colour motif, to soften it into having a more good humoured appearance.

'People sometimes accuse me of being seduced by materials and I do indeed love to make marks on glaze to see what happens when they are fired – that risk I enjoy taking. Painting is in some ways easier because the marks made remain the same, whereas with glaze there is always this tonal problem of working with something which appears pale green to start with and yet emerges from the kiln a shocking pink. But this unknown factor is very useful because it prevents me from treating the pots in too protective a manner, as often happens in painting. A potter has to come to terms with not knowing exactly how the piece is going to turn out until after firing. If the individual work becomes too precious to me then I think it shows, it has a stand-offish look.'

Through continual assessment of his work Archie has eventually built up a personal repertoire of imagery which he hopes other people can respond to:

'If we make objects which are so personal that they exclude all else then no one will understand them and we should not be surprised if no one is interested in them. It is the touching of others through my work which interests me most.'

Technical information

Clay body

55% Hyplas '71
27.5% grolleg
12.5% quartz
   5% potash feldspar

This body was designed, and is mixed, by Donald Logie, Errol, Perthshire, Scotland.

Glaze recipes

There are some basic glaze recipes which I find useful, but they can often be modified for particular results.

White

73% cornish stone
 9.5% whiting
 5.5% talc
10.5% china clay
 1.5% bone ash

Tenmoku

80% potash feldspar
 6% whiting
14% flint
 8% red iron oxide
 2% bentonite

Celadon *(from Bill Brown)*

33% feldspar
33% flint
17% china clay
17% whiting
 1.5% red iron oxide

Copper red

55% potash feldspar
22% whiting
 4% lead bisilicate
14% quartz
 3% tin oxide
 2.5% copper carbonate

Blue *(from John Glick)*

54% potash feldspar
13% whiting
 2.5% barium carbonate
 6% china clay
22.5% flint
 2.5% zinc oxide
 1.5% bentonite

plus rutile 1%, red iron 2%, cobalt oxide 0.5%

'The majority of my colours for decorating are produced by mixing a selection of oxides and stains into the basic white glaze. I started by mixing them in quantities between 10% and 25% but now do it mostly by eye. Additionally any other glaze or colourant is fair game for pouring or brushing, many of which may be disastrous on their own, but over or under other glazes, or in a small quantity may provide excellent results.'

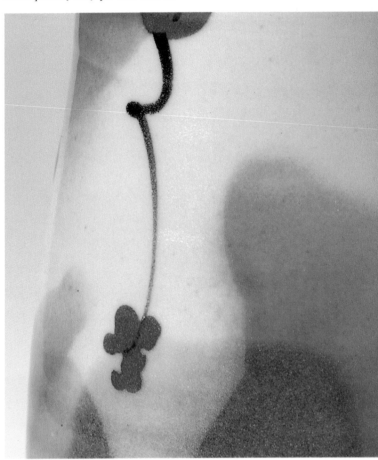

Detail of surface quality.

(Opposite) *Background*: Two handled vases, glazed white with blue and copper red glaze pours, brushwork in green, black and blue. 8½ inches high.
Foreground: thrown and manipulated oval dish glazed in white, blue and copper red, latex resist central motif in black, brushwork in black, green and blue. 9 inch diameter.

All photographs by Jonathan Robertson.

Gallery

Elaine Coleman (USA)
Incised porcelain jar, approx.
13 × 7 inches. Blue/green celadon
glaze leaf decoration, cone 10.
(Photos: Rick Paulson)

Incised green celadon teapot
(9 × 10½ inches, with handle). Leaf
design porcelain, cone 10.

Clive Davies (UK)
Stoneware jug, 6½ inches high.

Stoneware teapot 6¼ inches high. White base glaze, coloured glazes applied with slip trailer and brush.

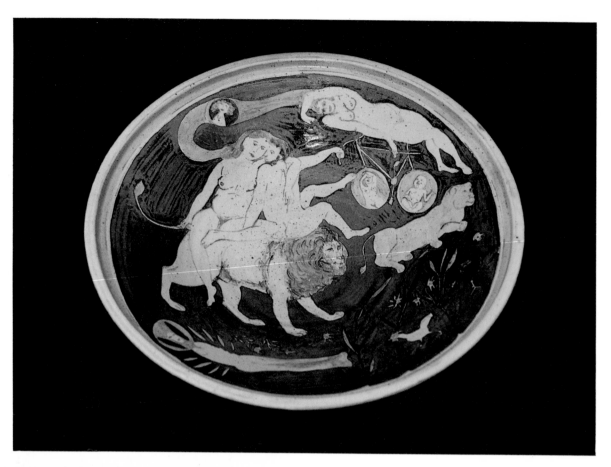

Eric James Mellon (UK)
Stoneware bowl, 14 inch diameter. Theme of tenderness with lions.
Reduction fired, ash glazed with oxide decoration, painted directly
onto biscuited pot before pouring the glaze.
(Photos: Anthony Hebdon)

Brush and watercolour drawings of lions from observation at
Murwell zoo.

Left: brush and watercolour composition for ceramic decoration.

Jenny Lind (USA)
Porcelain platter, 24 inches. Underglaze stains with china paint.

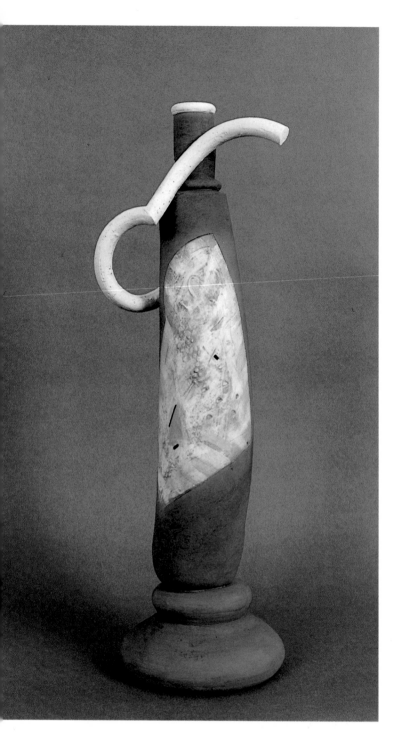

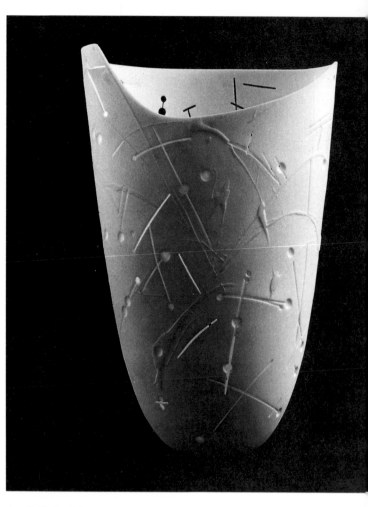

Angela Verdon (UK)
Bone china form with semi-piercings, piercings, incisions and applied slip. First firing to 1120°C, pierced, sanded with wet and dry paper then refired to 1220°C with a two hour soak. (Photo: John Coles)

David Scott (UK)
Blue vase, thrown and hand built. Grogged (molochite) white stoneware is used, or for more textured qualities heavy Crank clay. At the dry white stage a translucent porcelain slip is used which is under and overpainted with oxides, underglaze colours and slips, building up a rich and subtle surface. Fired to 1250°C, oxidised.

Andrew McGarva (UK)
Dish. Raw glazed wood fired stoneware (1300°C), with white glaze onglaze painting in iron cobalt and titanium oxide.

Kurt Weiser (USA)
Cast porcelain form, 18 × 5 × 10 inches, cone 10 reduction.

John Glick (USA)
Extruded and constructed box (10 inches × 10 inches wide, 6 inches high) Reduced stoneware. (Photo: Robert Vigiletti)

· 4 ·

Decorated salt glaze

In this section of the book we deal with the makers who use the process of salt glazing as a means of achieving a final glazed product. Salt glazing produces a marked effect on the surface of a pot both during and after firing, and this has to be considered in the making stages of a piece.

The glaze on the surface of the pot is created by the introduction of salt (usually common salt) into the combustion chamber or even the ware chamber of the kiln at various stages during the firing cycle. Kilns which use fossil based fuels, such as wood, oil, gas and coal are mainly used for salt glazing; electric kiln elements would deteriorate rapidly if exposed to salt vapour. Sodium chloride (salt) melts at around 800°C, yet if thrown into the kiln dry much of it would just form clinker in the base of the kiln — so to make it vapourise more rapidly the salt is mixed with a small amount of water. The heat of the kiln turns the water within the damp salt into super-heated steam, which helps the salt to decompose rapidly into the gases of sodium and hydrochloric acid. This volatile soda attacks the alumino-silicates present in the clay, and they combine to form sodium alumino-silicates, a type of glaze coating. For this reason, high silica content materials are best used to promote a fluid looking glaze — high alumina based materials retard or hinder the formation of a glaze, though this quality may be in fact used to some advantage when considering the surface decoration of a pot.

Volatilisation occurs after 1100°C, and continues until the clay reaches its vitrifying and maturing temperature, often between 1200°C and 1300°C. This particular process therefore falls within the high temperature ranges, although it has its own peculiarities.

In the past many fine works were produced by the salt glaze process. Because the finished work is hard and chemically resistant it has also been used for less inspiring items such as sewer pipes and acid storage jars. Contemporary salt glazers have moved away from these more mundane concerns using salt glaze to explore new effects and the four makers featured in this chapter are at the forefront of this field. Yet they all have to take into account certain physical changes which take place in the firing cycle. As the formation of the glaze coating depends on the mobile vapour permeating the kiln chamber by means of natural draughts and eddies, enclosed forms which the vapour cannot easily reach may need to have an ordinary glaze coating applied before firing. Any relief modelling, sgraffito or incised marking is accentuated by the salt glaze process. Slips, colours and any applied glazes are equally affected by the vapour, which alters any consciously applied decoration during the build-up of the glaze coating. The salt vapour softens the edges between slips and/or colours; and a characteristic feature of some types of salt glazed ware is that the glassy coating has the texture of orange peel.

In the work of Suzy and Nigel Atkins we see how incised and modelled surfaces are overlaid with layers of colours — this, combined with the salt glaze process, creates two particular kinds of surface texture. Anne Shattuck investigates ways of creating fluid colour effects by glazing over strongly spiralled handled vessels. The salt vapour adds an extra flux to the melting glaze, which flows and runs into the deep spiralled, incised lines of the pot, so that the work retains a fluent liquid quality when cooled. The illustrations of work by Michael Casson and Ruth King show pots which were fired in wood fuelled kilns — this means that ash deposits have melted on the surface of the pots, adding more colour and textural variations.

With Jane Hamlyn's work we see how free brushwork, impressed texture and subtle colours all coalesce in the firing process. Certainly what is apparent in the work of all the featured salt glazers is their skilful manipulation of a process which might initially seem to be restrictive and binding. As their work becomes more widely known we are now seeing a growing interest in a technique which was once used to produce sewer pipes!

Opposite: Teapot, Jane Hamlyn.

Jane Hamlyn

Visiting a local adult education institute in Battersea which offered both pottery classes and a creche for her two small children was the first step Jane Hamlyn took to becoming a potter. She attended adult classes for a number of years and eventually met Dan Arbeid on a summer course – he was the first teacher who took her work seriously, and after this Jane began to look around for full-time pottery courses, wanting the kind of training which would enable her to become a self-sufficient studio potter. As her two children were then of school age, in 1972 Jane enrolled on a full-time two year studio ceramics course at Harrow College, taking a job as a waitress to help with her finances.

Working restrictions in adult education classes, such as not enough time on the wheels, not much firing space, etc. and a compulsion to make pots had led Jane to make pinch pots and small modelled forms which could be produced at home. Her intrinsic love of the malleability of plastic clay dominated her first year at Harrow, and this awareness of the plastic nature of clay has grown and developed throughout her progress as a potter.

'The manipulative skills that come of learning to make pinch pots is something that has been with me ever since; I like working with clay in the soft rolling stage, when the clay is not too wet or too dry, but can be modelled and moulded to shape; finger and hand contact is at its most intimate at this point.'

After Harrow, where she had learned how to make thrown domestic ware efficiently, Jane went to work at

fellow student Peter Starkey's workshop and salt glazing techniques became paramount in her work.

'I was hooked on the concept and effects of salt glaze and my husband Ted was captivated by the kiln, the way it fired and its function, and expressed a willingness to take on that aspect of the work.'

By 1976 both Jane and Ted felt confident enough to search for a pottery of their own. Eventually they found a place in Everton, Nottinghamshire which had few neighbours and was ideal for salt glazing. Here the first kiln was designed and built by Jane and Peter Starkey. With Ted firing the kiln and Jane making the pots some good results emerged.

The earliest attempts at decoration was simply by dipping pots into various coloured slips and raw glazes, and many of the technical details and procedures were learned by trial and error.

'Although I have been inhibited about drawing and do not keep a formal sketchbook I believe that it is possible to draw with other things, e.g. a pair of scissors – it need not be a pencil. Very often the decision as to where to dip a pot in a slip or glaze is a form of drawing.

Jane's interest in manipulating plastic clay became apparent in her early work in the innovative way in which handles and other additions were made and attached. A private collection of Mayan figurative ocarinas seen at The Museum of Mankind, Burlington House, London, before she went to Harrow had a profound influence upon her attitude to clay modelling. The two-piece press-moulded figures had elaborate clay additions in the form of earrings, necklaces etc. and the fresh immediate way in which the Mayan potters approached the working of clay additions became a continuous source of inspiration. One of the earliest handles Jane made consisted of two coils of clay wrapped around a pencil; this was an attempt at a personal statement, avoiding the pulled handle, which she felt to be something of a cliché.

As a natural progression from dipping and pouring slips and glazes, Jane began to mask out areas on her pots using paper as a resist, supporting her view that one can draw with a pair of scissors as well as a pencil. Using motifs from the immediate landscape around the pottery, paper was torn and cut to represent trees and fields, and laid across the surfaces of the pots. Layers of slips and glazes were poured and squirted from a slip trailer across the surface of the pots in a direct way, creating contrasting marks and further areas of interest. Where the poured edges met and overlapped, the resisted areas created varying layers of visual and physical texture. The rigidity of the paper cutout was further softened during the firing process by the salt vapour attacking and softening the edges, and the colours washing over the surface decoration, muting the otherwise harsh-edged paper resist pattern. Certain areas were specially selected when packing the kiln. From experience Jane knew how much salt vapour would act in those areas and what degree of softening by the salt vapour would take place on the surface decoration.

After working through a range of ideas with paper resist images, Jane stopped using this technique as she felt the effect was becoming predictable, and this decorative line was not leading towards any new areas of stimulation. However, the next stage in Jane's decorative journey stemmed directly from the technique of using a slip trailer to squirt glaze across the surface of the paper resist patterns. Jane realised that there were qualities within a line of glaze, trailed or squirted across the pot's surface and this led to the 'squirt and dot' period of her decoration. Using coloured glazes, slip trailed and dotted on the pot's surface, gave a much freer quality to the decoration, each of the two marks, splash and dot, having different qualities. The dot made a focus for the eye which formalised the pattern.

For Jane this approach also became a little trite after a while; the lines and dots began appearing as bunches of grapes upon a vine, which she felt was too literal. Over a period of time the use of the slip trailer became more controlled and her interest was directed to the effects of glazes trailed upon the surface when salt reacts with them. Using glaze instead of slip gave a different quality. Because the glaze melts, a flatter, more subtle line is created, with iron pigment migrating to the edges of the trailed lines, reacting with the salt and creating a darker outline. This interaction between the application of glazes and slips and the way in which the salt vapour modifies and alters the qualities of the decoration became an increasingly important part of Jane's development. By simplifying the application of the decoration more colour could be introduced, and gradually a natural flowing line began to emerge.

'Grand Casserole number 2', 1985. 17¾ inches wide. Blue slip, lustrous green splashes. Heavily salt glazed.

113

Increasingly colour became a feature of Jane's decoration; white slip was used as a ground to give the coloured, trailed glazes greater resonance. The natural progression from using a white ground was to use a paler clay, porcelain.

Responding to the fine, dense qualities of porcelain clay, the quality of the pots became more refined. Using Japanese stencil motifs, Jane made and used carved bisque stamps, to impress the leatherhard, dense white surface of the porcelain clay. More delicate colours were dipped and trailed upon the surface; the overall effect was primarily floral. As the forms became more refined and thinner in section Jane realised that to apply soft modelled handles would distort the shapes, so she consciously manipulated and altered the forms to accommodate the modelled handles. This gave rise to a floral 'frilly' effect on the tops of the vessels as they were pushed and altered whilst wet.

All this happened over a number of years and during that time Jane became dissatisfied with the way in which the work was developing; her feeling was that it was becoming too pretty and precious.

'I like looking at the finer details in work from other disciplines such as carving, painting, embroidery, etc. but I became so involved in the personal, intimate, finer details of ceramic quality, in the impressed marks, dipped areas, trailing and modelled handles of my pots that the forms and overall body of work was drawing away from me; much of the strength I had in my stoneware was getting lost.'

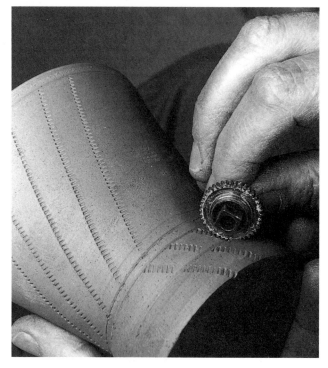

1 Above left: A rib is used to make a broad spiral up the base of a pot.

2 Above right: The rim is distorted ready for the handle.

3 Below right: A cog from a child's clockwork toy is used to impress a fine textured line.

To counteract this unwanted 'sweetness' in her work, Jane stopped using the porcelain and returned to stoneware. Her present work consolidates the strengths of previous forms and she has re-evaluated the decorative techniques developed during the making of her porcelain.

'If you make a lot of intricate decoration the form needs to be simple, and if you get carried away with the decoration the form can slip away from you without you noticing it; it is so easy to lose your way without realising what is happening.'

Jane uses two different types of clay in her present production; a fine, pale, porcellanous stoneware is used for smaller pieces, and it also makes a strong teapot body. The second clay is a mix, with the addition of sand to increase the particle size, and promote the 'orange peel' surface quality which occurs when the salt vapour reacts with the larger particles of silica. Many of the large forms and the ovenware is made of this sandy-textured clay. The orange peel effect can be carried more successfully on a larger scale, whereas orange peel surface on smaller pots may seem out of proportion with the scale of the piece.

Jane's work begins as thrown vessels. Whilst the pot is on the wheel the shape is worked and altered using a rib to give movement and fluidity to the line of the pot's profile, distorting and establishing divisions for decoration and handles within the shape of the piece. Design decisions are made on the wheel as the pot is being formed, giving a spontaneity and individual quality to each pot made, partly through the sense of discovery and partly by allowing things to take their own course. Handles are formed in a number of ways, beginning with the extrusion of coils of clay. The handles are variously modelled and manipulated to give each one an individual textured surface. Handles of

4 Above left: Rolling the mug handle on a textured surface to create pattern and texture.

5 Below: Attaching the handle.

6 Sections of rubber car mat and the patterns they create on extruded clay handles.

differing thickness are rolled on textured rubber matting (car mats) or rolled with a wooden ruler to give a spiralling line. These are then attached in a direct manner to the leatherhard pots and some are finished by stamping with the carved biscuit stamps. Using a roulette (a cog from a child's metal robot) Jane marks the surface of the pot with delicate and subtle lines of rouletting. Part or whole of the pot is then dipped in a variety of slips and glazes, which lays down the first layer of colour. Over this layer Jane uses wide brushes to sweep a second coloured slip across the pot with bold strokes. This strong, bold approach to the decorative process supports the intense treatment given to the pot during the salt firing – the surface is attacked and changed by the salt vapour, sometimes obliterating, sometimes highlighting the marks made upon the surface of the pot.

Much of Jane's success in producing strong harmonious work relies on the separate elements relating to each other in a sympathetic manner. Her awareness of design is now very much linked with what best lends itself to the process of salt glazing. Strong forms are married with bold brushed colour, the soft modelled quality of the handles all highlighted by the action of salt vapour, resulting in a body of work which is thoughtfully made and sensitively finished.

7 Using a circular sponge to roll pigment onto a mug.

8 Some carved stamps to impress designs into clay.

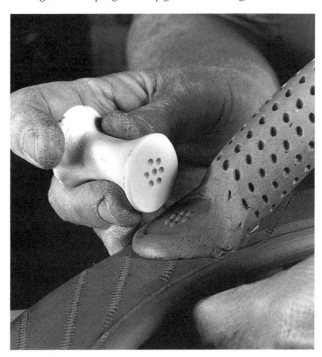

9 A handle is attached to the rim of a pot using the biscuit fired stamp.

Opposite: Jug, 1985, 10½ inches high. Pale body clay, blue slip and green brushed decoration. Textured, modelled handle.

10 Slip is applied to a large casserole, with the wheel slowly turning, using a wide brush giving a broad, free brushmark.

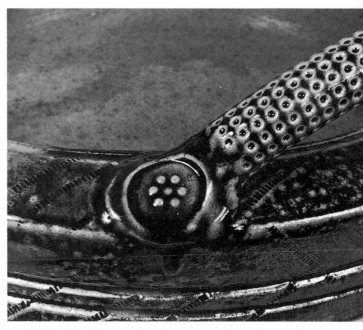

Detail of fired bowl, showing how the glaze emphasises the stamping, texture of handle and marks made by the cog wheel.

'Dark Casserole', 1985, 11¾ inches wide. Roulette decoration, green brushmarks. Blue slip – slightly 'undersalted', i.e. fired in a more sheltered position within the kiln.

Technical information

Clay body
1½ bags s.m.d. ball clay
½ bag moira plastic stoneware
10% sand

White slip
50% s.m.d. ball clay
50% china clay

Blue slip
50% nepheline syenite
50% ball clay
to this add
1.5% cobalt oxide
10% rutile

Shino raw glaze
10 parts nepheline syenite
4 parts a.t. ball clay

Photography by John Coles.

Green raw glaze
24% potash feldspar
18% whiting
30% a.t. ball clay
30% quartz
5% red iron oxide

Mixture for wadding mix
2 lb alumina hydrate
8 ozs china clay
4 ozs ball clay
4 ozs grog dust
4 ozs flour (makes the mixture 'plastic' but goes mouldy if kept)

Wide, low, serving dish. 15¾ inches wide. Textured handles and impressed stamps. Shino glaze liner. 1985.

Anne Shattuck

'Working in clay was not an active choice, it just happened, and I liked it immediately. It was a material that no one seemed to be overly serious about and I thought, well, this is for me! I became very excited about the potential of this new-found material, and put all else aside to learn about it.'

Putting all else aside, Anne Shattuck came to England to study pottery at Harrow College. With Mick Casson heading a team of dedicated potters, the training at Harrow at that time tended to follow an apprenticeship approach to pot-making, though the students did not necessarily have to perform the menial tasks associated with a traditional workshop apprenticeship. Repetition making of objects and the strong prevailing work ethic gave Anne a firm grounding in technique, which later allowed her the freedom to explore the aesthetic concerns of form and decoration.

'I soon discovered clay had wonderful qualities. It could take almost any shape or be manipulated with a variety of techniques. It could be transformed into something as useful as a bowl, or as thought-provoking as a huge sculpture. A lot of talk was given to technique and process when I was learning about clay, and for good reason – unless you understand what you are doing with clay your thoughts will never come to fruition. Clay is not meant for the frail spirit, it takes incredible energy and unfailing commitment to make it work for you. You must develop a deep relationship with this material or be undermined by its very nature.'

Many of Anne's forms and decorative motifs have a quality and simplicity which is reminiscent of folk art. Her forms have strong presences which offer a sense of permanence, whilst her colours and brushwork are lively, free and bright, flowing across the surface of her work in a fluid, vibrant way.

'A lot of my work borrows explicitly from folk art; a guilt-free way of decorating which says "forget the rules, let your spirit come through". I want to put a liveliness and a spirit into my work as well as an energy and a strength and a power. My pots are about growth; I would almost like to plant them in the earth and have them look natural there.'

Anne's more recent work has been carried out in porcelain clay, which gives a brilliant white background for her colours and motifs. The wet fluid appearance of the freshly made pieces is accentuated and given permanence through the salt glaze firing that she adopts because each mark, and both texture and line are highlighted by the reaction of the sodium vapour with the silica in the slips and glazes. Anne feels that porcelain gives a certain presence to the fired pots that is not found with other clays, a quality that is cool, hard and almost indestructible. Her recent porcelain work has been an attempt to capture the feeling and gesture of motion – clay spinning on the wheel, the movement of brushstrokes over the clay's surface, and the wild, intense activity of salt firing, all three stages contributing to the finished look of the work.

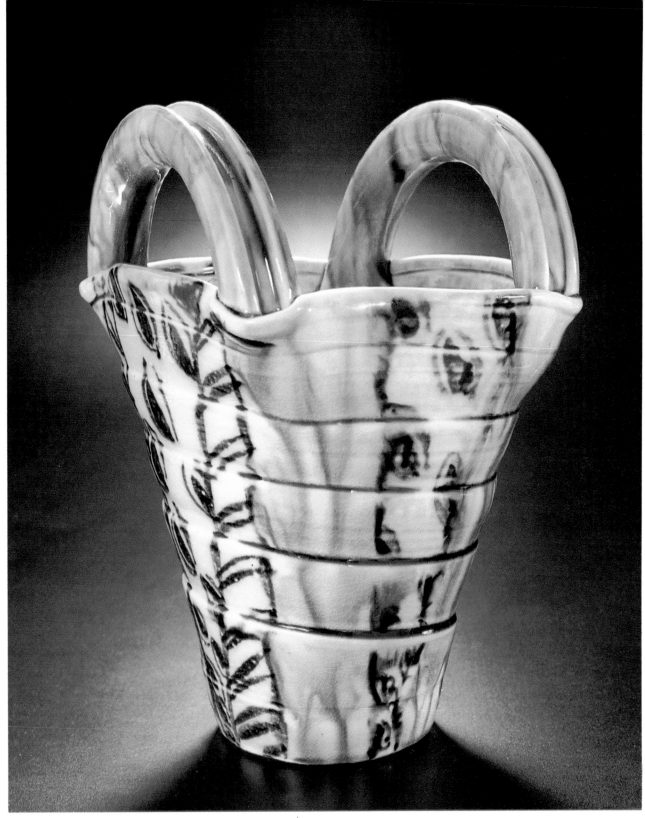

Salt glazed porcelain basket, 1983, 14 × 7 × 6 inches.

'I do not separate the idea of decoration from the act of making. It is not something that just sits on the final surface but includes the forming of the pot and the firing.'

Almost all of Anne's work is wheel thrown and this forming method suits the pots she makes, as she places emphasis upon spiral motion and the growth of dynamic lines within the structure of the pieces. Her pots based on the basket form have a layered, almost wrapped feel to them, spiralling and growing upwards. They remain completely functional as baskets but deal with interesting visual concepts. She often leaves deep throwing marks on pots to exaggerate the wheel-formed process, achieved by using a large sharp rib on the pot to give the piece a 'wrapped' look. Alternatively, on shallow pots such as her 'ocean basket' series the outside of the pot is smoothed out, contrasting with the heavily marked interior.

After a pot has been worked on the wheel it is allowed to dry just to the point where it can be handled without collapsing. It is then trimmed and reassessed to see how it might develop. Many of Anne's forms are altered and re-shaped at this stage; her tall forms are often squared off at the top and pushed out at the base; the flat open pots are ovaled off and the edges are pinched and squeezed. The continual exploration and manipulation of clay forms at this stage gives an organic quality and feel to the pots, expressive of Anne's feelings about our contemporary environment.

'At a time when I see so much stress and anxiety, such a lack of beauty and a loss of hope around me, I want to put good energy back into the world with my pots.'

Coils are extruded to act as the basis for appendages such as handles. These coils are given the same kind of treatment as the main forms, being paddled, pulled and pressed into lively, interestingly soft organic shapes, and each set of coils is made exclusively for each pot.

2 Extruding a square shape for the basis of a handle.

1 Almost all the work is initially wheel thrown and later altered into asymmetrical forms.

3 Softening the angles on the extrusion and creating new lines with the thumb.

After the handles have been satisfactorily attached the pot is allowed to dry slowly under plastic. When the work is totally dry it is biscuit fired. Anne does not once-fire her work because of the large scale of some of her pieces – also the work may go through multiple glazing and decorative stages and it is handled a great deal too, so she feels that decorating is easier with biscuit fired ware.

Glazing is the middle stage of her decorative process; she uses a combination of brushwork, slip techniques and glazes, all of which is done with the salt glazing process in mind. During firing the salt vapour will soften the glazed edges and brushwork, attacking and altering images and highlighting the form. The glazes react with the salt vapour, melting, running and pooling into the ribs and finer marks, accentuating and exaggerating their existence. Usually Anne sets aside a few weeks for glazing her pots – she needs to immerse herself totally in this part of the process, as it is so important to envisage how the glazes will react with the salt vapour during firing. She begins by lining up all her biscuit fired pots on tables in the studio and reviewing them carefully. Then when decisions have been made about how to treat the surfaces all the washes, slips and glazes are made ready for use.

4 The final twisting and shaping of a handle.

5 Attaching the handle to pot.
All size pots are made from small 10–12 inch baskets to baskets over 36 inches.

The choice of brush is important in order to produce the variety of strokes she wants. Long stemmed hakes in many widths are used for the broad strokes and sumi-styled calligraphy brushes are used for the fine detail. The detailed areas are worked upon first using frit, plus a stain or oxide and water for a wash; after the brushwork is complete slips are applied where controlled, bold, denser colour is needed. Then to give spontaneity and fluidity to the overall surface she highlights and layers with cone 9 glazes. None of the decoration is arbitrarily applied – after much trial and error Anne has learned how the materials will react with each other and with the salt vapour during firing.

The final stage of the decoration is the salt firing. Anne has worked with this type of glaze firing for ten years and after many struggles has made it work for her, manipulating the firing cycle and using salt vapour as one would use

6 Left: Attaching extruded and handbuilt handles to tall basket forms.

7 Decorating a pot with stains, glazes and slips. A fine calligraphy brush is used for detail work.

any other tool. She is constantly reappraising every aspect of her work, and she takes particular notice of what happens during the salt firing, where the volatile and vaporous atmosphere can lift some of the oxides and stains from their original place and redeposit them elsewhere. Many of the surface areas are purposefully left white so that the activity during firing can be caught and recorded; pink, blue and green blushes are not unusual, as well as the orange peel quality often seen in salt glazed work.

'I am rarely satisfied with what I make, but I keep struggling and plodding along, knowing that each pot evolves into another and that I am as honest with clay as I can be; my work continues to grow and I feel satisfaction from that; when you are on the right path your heart leads the way.'

8 Salting the salt kiln. Salt is put into fireboxes with an angle iron attached to a a metal bar. Goggles and mask are always worn during the salting.

9 Firing the salt kiln. An exhilarating but exhausting process.

Anne's thorough knowledge of materials and her firing process and her spirited approach to decoration all contribute to a body of work which is lively and colourful – and she has strong feelings about what it is to be a potter today:

'Beyond the day to day business of running a studio and living my life I have a sense of being a link in a very long chain. For thousands of years and in every civilisation there have been clay workers; potters have brought a basic material to life and in doing so have shown us much about their particular culture; I cannot help but wonder what historians will think when they look at ours.'

'Flower basket', 18 inches high, salt glazed porcelain.

Opposite: 'Wrapped basket', salt-glazed porcelain. 20 inches high.

'Clam serving dish', salt glazed porcelain, 18 inches diameter.

(Photos: Jim Bailey)

Technical information

The following recipes I have used successfully on porcelain for the past few years, and they yield a wide spectrum of colours for oxidised to neutral salt firings.

Slips

White
18% china clay
20% light ball clay
25% flint
30% nepheline syenite
7% borax frit

Pink
75% nepheline syenite
25% china clay
17% 6075 manganese alumina pink stain

Orange
25% china clay
25% flint
25% whiting
25% luster spar
10% nepheline syenite
2% titanium
15% saturn orange stain 6121 (CR FE 2n AL)
10% vanadium stain 6404 (Sn v)

Iridescent
50% china clay
50% ball clay
20% rutile
30% nepheline syenite

Direct brush decoration:
Stain/frit: 4/1 + water to a wash consistency (ferro frit 3124)
I add Mason stains, listed below, for a variety of colour results.

Mason Stains

Number	Name	Analysis	Amount	Colour Produced
6302	Cadet Blue	CR Co Al Si Sn	15%	light blue
6371	Dark Teal	CR Co Al	20%	dark green
6483	Parseodymium	Pr Zr V	8%	yellow
6003	Crimson	CR Sn	38%	raspberry (add frit)
6003	Crimson	CR Sn	28%	dark rose
6404	Vanadium	Sn V	13%	
6385	Pansy Purple	Cr Sn Co	15%	lavender

Glaze

For shiny salt glaze outside and inside, with orange peel effect.

Base glaze
14% china clay
16% potash feldspar
17% soda feldspar
31% flint
2% zinc
17% whiting
3% dolomite

To colour the base glaze I add the following stains:

Purple	add 15% Pansy Purple stain
Sea green	add 15% Dark Teal stain
Orange/green	add 15% Saturn Orange stain
Green	add 15% French Green stain

To obtain fluid glazes for accents where I want a runny effect I use the following.

Blue
25% china clay
25% whiting
25% flint
25% potash feldspar
15% nepheline syenite
1% cobalt
7% rutile (light milled)
(apply thinly)

Yellow
42% potash feldspar
21% flint
16% whiting
9% china clay
9% red iron
2% zinc oxide
8% nepheline syenite
(apply thickly)

I use Crowells Black for fine line brushwork and blanket coverage.

Suzy and Nigel Atkins

Suzy and Nigel Atkins set up their salt glaze pottery near Montsalvy in the Auvergne in 1977. Concentrating only on functional ware they have built up an international reputation based upon a consistently high quality of craftsmanship and the extraordinary richness of the fired surfaces. Their work currently draws some ten thousand visitors a year to the remote valley where the bulk of their production is sold. Suzy makes and decorates the work while Nigel is responsible for firing and maintaining the kiln and looking after the business administration.

When they first started the work was all simple thrown ware with a simple coating of slip. The slips were those developed when Suzy was at Harrow College and they were left to interact as best they might with the La Borne clay that now lay underneath them. The kiln was a three cubic metre downdraught blockhaus they built themselves and the gentle rhythm of the firings meant that progress was slow. It took two full years to develop other slips better adapted to the French clay and to get to grips with the salt firings.

In 1980 Suzy started to decorate her work, using finger wipes and combing in simple direct patterns with slip trailing applied to accentuate the principle rhythms or to provide a contrasting geometric structure. As the techniques developed so the pots changed as well. Forms to be decorated were smoothly ribbed while those destined solely to be slipped were reappraised to see how a decorative surface could be given to them whilst still wet on the wheel.

A memorable series of large hexagonal boxes and tall jugs produced in 1982 brought together these two approaches with great panache – but the conflict of the thrown and distorted surfaces, the wild rhythms of the impressed rings and scratches set against the dribbled slip trailing placed these works at the outer limits of the Baroque. The way forward had to be by other means.

The first step was a return to the drawing board, not to re-examine the shapes of the pots (which Suzy has always developed through working directly on the wheel) but to put some organisation into the decorated surfaces so that they could contain something more than directional energy. From winter watercolour studies came (in 1983) a long series of fine, large pots, nearly all lidded, glowing with rich friezes of pictograms of the natural world— flowers, butterflies, trees and clouds set in contrast with the tight patterns of man's organisation; fences, grilles, paving, brickwork barriers. These elements were not chosen (as some might think) to impart an ecological message but purely for graphic impact. The layout of the geometric elements was the most direct way of organising the surface of the pot, at the same time providing both foil and filter for the natural elements to be laid out later. The butterfly could fight with the net or float free, the cloud could be seen through a garden fence or drift overhead, shedding, if needed, a shaft of fine pointillist rain. This simple juxtaposition of the inert, of the free with the fixed, introduced a new tension into the designs.

Simultaneously the firing cycle was also being reviewed and experiments with controlled fast cooling to 1000°C were beginning to give exciting results. For reasons that are not at all clear Nigel was able to produce highly lustred surfaces with tints of copper, bronze, gold or silver depending on which slips or combinations of slips were used and where the pots were placed in the kiln. These results seem to be particular to the Le Don kiln, and the French government funded a research project in the winter of 1985 to see how a kiln could be constructed to produce these effects more regularly on all the pots. In 1983 Suzy also undertook a lot of experiments to determine the interaction of different slips, laying them on in layers in different sequences, slip trailing between the layers and studying the effects of double and treble dipping of various slips. The result of this work has been a palette of rich colours uncommon in most salt glazed ware, with which she has now been working for the last couple of years. Dense mallard greens glow brilliantly and break up into silver eyelets as the salting increases, a semi-matte brick-red turns through bronze and copper to hints of gold, a pale smokey blue/grey when set high in the kiln runs to sky-blue rimmed with rhodium lace, and a pale cinnamon cream blushes to peach before speckling with brown dots like the egg of a French moran.

Detail of decoration on large cache pot (now in the Collection Koch, USA). Bold wax resist design laid over broad areas defined with bands of paper resist. Note the tonal differences due to variations in attack by salt vapour. Simple motifs are accentuated with slip trailing, here giving striking results.

1–2 Freshly thrown clay is marked and scored, offering a rich visual and physical texture. The salt vapour will highlight this texture underneath the subsequent layers of decoration.

If the means of expression have matured and richened Suzy's artistic concerns have remained surprisingly constant:

'All my work is based upon functional pots; this is a conscious choice which we re-examine regularly but at present we can see no valid reason for moving towards purely decorative wares. On the contrary, both the symbolic and functional values of my work are very important and have been a major creative stimulus since the beginning. My pots are both a reflection and an affirmation of my need for a certain kind of caring domesticity. That they should be useful and used is vital and it gives me great pleasure to think of them participating daily in the lives of others.

My decoration is subordinate to this overall view of my work and is likely to remain so – however, the format of a decorative idea is often the determining factor in the choice of which pot will carry that decoration, the decision being made before the pot is thrown.'

3 A thickly thrown footring is sliced and sculpted, using a bent wire.

4–5 Added feet are modelled and textured using a variety of tools, including wooden mouldings.

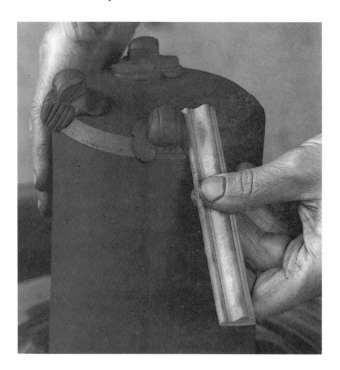

Opposite: Large flat plate, c. 19 inch diameter. Basic kaolin slip is applied to leatherhard pot. Overall design is set out in soft pencil on paper, pattern is cut. When the pot is bone dry, red areas are masked out with paper and the slip is applied. Wax resist is then brushed on to make blue and kaolin slip, red slip is then applied, and sgraffito work and slip trailing added. The rim is textured when the plate is thrown and then painted with red slips when dry.

Opposite: Example of a small area finely worked with sgraffito. A grid is laid out with slip trailing; after this paper resist is applied, and then protected from the red slip with a wax coat.

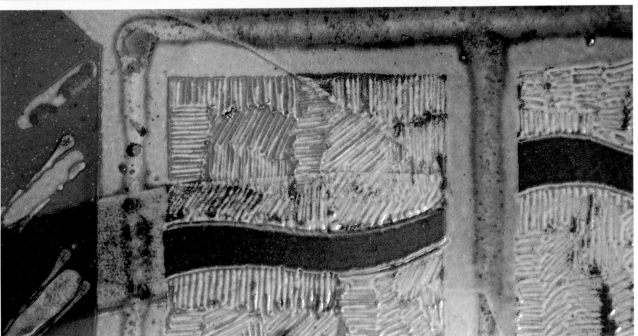

Technical information

Clay
La Borne stoneware clay – Terres et cendres du Borry

Kiln
3 cubic metre propane gas fired, using 20 kilograms of salt, with pots raw glazed and single fired to 1320°C. Crash cooled from 1320 to 1000°C, with a firing cycle of 30 hours.

Slips
Basic kaolin slip
50% kaolin
50% hyplas 71 ball clay

Red slip semi-matt
70% kaolin
30% a.t. ball clay

Blue slip

70% nepheline syenite
 5% a.t. ball clay
25% hyplas 71 ball clay
 1% cobalt carbonate

Slip trailing mixture
90% powdered porcelain
10% nepheline syenite

To this mixture 10% of the following commercial stains are added: rosepink, yellow, orange, victoria green, mazarine blue. These stains are obtained from Pottery Crafts.

Iron rich slip
36% a.t. ball clay
21% potash feldspar
27% silica
16% whiting
 4% red iron oxide

Pair of teapots c. 4 inch diameter. The same techniques used as for the large plate. Note the different textures in the sgraffito work and metallic lustering from the firing. The slip trailing over mallard green is in an iron rich slip which has the effect of fluxing the top slip coat to show the one below.

All photography by Pierre Soissons.

Gallery

Michael Casson (UK)
Right: Vase, 30 inches high. Iron bearing clay, with successive layers of poured white slip, builds up the colour variation that results from salt and ash acummulation on the surface during firing. Cobalt stains, ash glaze on the inside and brushed on the outside.

Ruth King (UK)
Below: Wood fired salt glaze stoneware, 10 inches high. Inlaid porcelain in geometric pattern with spots of blue slip. Slab-built clay 50/50 Ivanhoe + St Thomas.

· 5 ·

Onglaze decoration

In this final chapter we look at onglaze decoration, which comes in two main forms, enamels and metal lustres. Lustres are thin metallic surfaces which fuse to the glaze, made by adding metals in chloride form to sodium resinate and suspending these in oil so that they can be applied easily. Various thicknesses can be achieved by using thinners. Lustres are not usually made by potters themselves, but are bought prepared from manufacturers. Enamels are soft firing glazes, which can be both transparent and opaque; again, potters usually buy enamels ready prepared but in this chapter Russell Coates describes how he makes his own enamels, with methods derived from his own research and his training in Japan. Although different in chemical composition, both substances are generally applied to a previously fired piece, which is then fired again at a lower temperature than the work was first subjected to, so that the first glaze layer remains undisturbed.

Traditionally onglaze techniques were the only way to obtain bright colours in ceramics, made possible by the lower temperatures of the final firing, which allows stability in compounds which are very volatile at higher temperatures. As we have seen, vibrant yet stable colour is now possible at high temperatures as a result of recent technical developments with the commercial preparation of clay, glazes, and underglazes. Yet because of the particular qualities of enamels and lustres, their visual and tactile density and the richness they can lend to a design, integrating and bonding with previously fired glazes, makers are still using a final firing to conclude the process of vessel making.

Some of the makers whose work is illustrated in this chapter use onglaze colours in addition to the main emphasis of their decoration, using them to focus on elements within the form or on the surface qualities in their work. Other potters use onglaze colours as the main form of decoration. Not all onglaze techniques need to be applied over a previously fired glaze: Judy Trim often uses lustres over burnished unglazed ware, so that when fired the lustres eat into the soft ceramic surface of the relatively low fired body, offering different intensities and interesting iridescent, fading colours. In contrast, John Wheeldon's use of colour and lustre is highly finished, with rigidly structured patterns, stamped on the hard high-fired glaze of his bowls. Mary Rich's work is also very structured in design, and she uses strong colour combinations.

Both David Taylor and Patrick Loughran use the further low firing to highlight elements of their work in bold colour, David Taylor using enamels and Patrick Loughran lustres. Russell Coates, Alan Peascod, Jamie McCrae and Paul Mathieu create complex patterns and effects with enamels or with lustres. Geoffrey Swindell uses lustres in an unusual way. He builds up layers of lustres and breaks up the surface tension of the lustre medium before it has dried on the pot by squirting paraffin or detergent onto the pot between the layers. This creates interesting visual texture and rich colours.

Roger Michell (UK)
Thrown and turned jar. Black underglaze colour is sponged on, then a low solubility glaze follows. Gold lustre in laquer form is thinly sponged on pot.

Russell Coates

Russell Coates' decision to study in Japan came about through a combination of things – his developing ideas and experiments in ceramic techniques and firing ranges and a keen interest in Oriental pottery and porcelain. After his initial instruction in painting and sculpture at Manchester and Portsmouth Art Schools from 1967 to 1971 it was three years before he returned to art training. Then from 1974 to 1975 he studied at Goldsmiths' College in south London, gaining an art teacher's certificate, and it was during this time that he discoverd an interest in pottery and became increasingly immersed in the aesthetic, scientific and technical aspects of claywork. He realised what a wide scope ceramics offered and that it gave him the possibility of making objects that could have artistic value which people could also enjoy using. With this in mind, Russell spent from 1975 to 1979 at Goldsmith's gaining an advanced diploma in ceramics, much valuable workshop experience, while teaching part-time in various adult education institutes, and was awarded a British Council/Japanese Government Mombusho Scholarship to study ceramics in Japan.

The first work that Russell produced reflected his earlier training in painting and sculpture – slab, pinch and coil techniques used mainly in vases and boxes. Later, when he started to throw, this method of production quickly became, and is still, the most important. He also uses press moulds, centred hump moulds and his most recent work shows a resurgent interest in slab-built pieces. During his training and the development of his workshop practice

Russell moved through the spectrum of firing temperatures; he began by making vases, planters and plates in earthenware, gradually moving into stoneware and finally to porcelain. Russell's interest and abilities in ceramics grew in conjunction with his interest in Japan – not only in ceramics but also in Japanese history and culture, art and architecture. Oriental glazes began to play an increasingly important role in the work Russell was making, particularly those glazes traditional to China and Japan – celadons, copper reds, tenmokus, chun etc. So the offer of a British Council/Japanese Government scholarship was clearly a great opportunity.

After six months on an intensive Japanese language course in Osaka, Russell was placed in a university. His first intention was to extend his knowledge of reduction fired stoneware and porcelain, but a chance to learn the techniques of enamelled porcelain came up, as he was offered a place at Kanazawa college of art and design, in the Ishikawa prefecture, under the tutelage of Professor Fujio Kitade. This was extremely fortunate as the area where the college is situated is particularly noted for its very skilled enamellers, Professor Kitade being one of the most esteemed in Japan. Historically the area was, and is still, famous for Kutani wares, and also for the production of underglaze blue wares. For Russell, in terms of his own development, introduction to the techniques of enamelled porcelain was a means of combining his early training as a painter with his skills as a potter.

138

Enamelled porcelain vase, 8½ inches high, 6¾ inch diameter.

From the beginning his training under Fujio Kitade was nothing if not thorough. A strict discipline was adhered to, and through exhaustive series of tests he gained respect for, and deep knowledge of, materials and techniques. Under Professor Kitade's watchful eye Russell learnt to pay great attention to the subtleties of the form, line and weight of the work in progress. For instance, his first task was to choose some fifty shapes from books illustrating pottery of the Jomon period and Yayoi wares to make accurate drawings of those pieces. From that selection of pots he had to choose one which he made many times over. When Professor Kitade was satisfied the pieces all had to be decorated in a wide variety of ways.

Concentrating on the traditional designs of enamelled porcelain obviously created rigid parameters to work within. Birds, flowers, fish, water and landscapes were copied from plates to vases and vice versa, the necessary rearrangement of design enabling Russell to gain a sure understanding of appropriate spacings and colour balances. The time came when Russell was asked to work on his own shapes and designs which then blossomed from his response to traditional Japanese landscapes. The discipline and close attention to technical detail he learned in his apprenticeship has stayed with him and has been equally important in the establishment and progress of his current work. He firmly established his skills in determining form and colour balance, brush control, assessing the thickness of enamels and the accurate marking out of designs.

Russell's scholarship was extended on the recommendation of his professor and this enabled him to work on translating Japanese materials into their British equivalents, thus duplicating the traditional colours with British raw materials, and also to have a very successful one-man show in Kanazawa city. Professor Kitade then arranged for him to gain workshop practice at the Toshioka porcelain works in Nomanchi, Kanazawa city, where provision was also made for him to continue his own work. Russell gained success and recognition for the work he produced, showing in prestigious venues and exhibitions, including the Ishikawa Prefecture Craft Exhibition and the Japanese New Craft Exhibition.

Russell returned to Britain to establish his present workshop in London in 1983. His present work retains an influence of Japan in terms of design and in execution, and is basically concerned with underglaze blue patterning under the porcelain glaze used in conjunction with brightly coloured overglaze enamels. The underglaze blue is made from metal oxides, as are all of Russell's pigments and the production of it is carefully controlled to offer optimum results.

Each batch of the blue pigment is made in 50 gram quantities and after thorough testing the preferred depth and shade of blue can be achieved. Underglaze blues vary and can contain more than fifteen different elements. Oxides such as cobalt, iron, manganese and nickel are combined and fired in an unglazed porcelain dish to a temperature of 1150°C; at this temperature the oxides sinter and fuse together, forming a hard homogenous clinker which has to be chipped from the porcelain dish after cooling. This clinker is then broken up with a large pestle and mortar to a roughly ground size and the gritty material is then reduced to a finely ground powder in an electrically driven pestle and mortar, though a small pestle and mortar will work just as well. Before application the calcined and powdered oxides are further ground or mulled on a glass plate using a porcelain muller and mixed with the liquid strained from an infusion of green tea. Mixing the green tea liquid with the pigment gives a drying strength and allows the underglaze blue pigment to flow and adhere to the biscuited pot. By the same process underglaze iron and underglaze copper red may be produced – Russell has in fact used all of these colours but underglaze blue prevails in his present production.

His underglaze blue motifs began by being traditionally Japanese in concept and application – peonies, chrysanthemums, fish and lattice work, all fired under a transparent glaze. But more recently his designs have developed along much more abstract lines, while still reflecting his affinity with natural themes – fields, rocks, sky, river and land formations.

'I have always found fascinating the contrast between the organic patterning of nature and the geometry man introduces when moulding the landscape. This is particularly noticeable in Japan where, for example, architecture is often composed of pure geometric shapes, dark beams forming a series of rectangles, white squares of plaster, triangular roofs and circular stepping stones across garden ponds. Agriculture, too, has altered their environment with a geometric grid of rice fields which is in direct contrast with the soaring mountains and bamboo forests.'

Russell's source materials for designs extend to the very materials used in making pots – the essential structures of rocks and glasses that form the basis of all ceramics are used to create patterns and images in his work. Exploring this field Russell collects images of, for example, the microscopic patterning of rocks and crystals. Strong contrasts are created; patterns drawn from the appearance of water, forest and field are combined with those derived from snow and rock crystals, and the imagery which results is of contrasting harmonies, subtly balanced.

'I use patterns which range from the simple motif which repeats itself regularly to patterns which may emerge from a more irregular source, such as light on water, which is broken down into elements whose relationship with each other is constantly changing yet still intimately tied.'

Many of the designs are established early on in the underglaze blue stage. After biscuit firing (to 800°C for Japanese porcelain clays, and 1000°C for British porcelain) the pots are first immersed in water for approximately thirty seconds and then allowed to stand for around three minutes; this is to offset some of the porosity of the biscuited pots which if not soaked will 'drag' at the brush, sucking in the pigment and not allowing the colour to flow along the surface. At this stage decisions have to be made about the early structure of the design; what will be done in underglaze blue and how this will combine with the onglaze enamels to be applied later. Some of Russell's pots don't in fact have any underglaze decoration, all the designs being made during the onglaze enamel stage.

Russell uses a clear lime-balanced alkaline glaze, termed a white glaze in Japan, over the biscuited pots, applied to a thickness of approximately 0.4 mm when underglaze decoration is used. Pots which are destined only for enamel decoration may have a slightly thicker glaze coating, however. An even coating of glaze is extremely important and much time and effort is spent achieving this, even soaking the slightly thicker areas of pots with water to prevent excessive build-up of glaze on those areas. Often enclosed forms such as vases are glazed on the inside first before the underglaze blue is applied, so that the glaze won't spill onto the decoration; it is difficult, if not impossible, to eradicate mistakes in application of the glaze over the underglaze painting.

The glaze firing takes place in a gas-fired kiln over approximately fourteen hours, to a temperature equivalent to Orton cone 9, and with a reduction atmosphere from 960°C to 1240°C, the heaviest reduction being at about 1100°C, the kiln finishing with a neutral atmosphere. The reduction plays an important role in the final colours of the pots; too much oxygen and the piece takes on a yellowish, creamy tint – too little oxygen and the pots take on a greyish hue.

Preparation for onglaze enamelling begins with making a solution of gelatine which comes in the form of a barley sugar-like stick to use as a cleaning agent, removing any dust and grease and acting as a coating on the glaze fired pot. First a small amount of hard, brittle gelatine is broken off and then boiled in a small amount of water until a solution is made of the correct viscosity. One test of the viscosity is to smear some of the solution on the hands and to clap them together – if the hands stick slightly then the correct thickness has been achieved. The gelatine solution is wiped over the glaze surface producing a thin coat which gives the otherwise shiny glaze a very slightly matt coating which allows any brush painting to flow across the pot, depositing an even line of pigment.

2 Diluted underglaze blue is used as a wash.

3 Pot with underglaze blue, pigment and brushes.

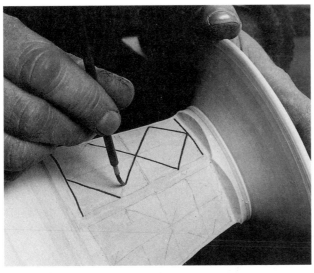

1 The design is first drawn on the biscuited pot in pencil and then outlined in underglaze blue.

4 Above left: The enamel pigment of porcelain mullers and paint brushes are stored on glass sheets in the enamels box.

5 Above right: A design can be painted directly onto paper using a ground charcoal solution.

6 Below left: Patterns can be made for specific pots or selected from those in the pattern book.

7 Below right: The charcoaled paper can then be used to paint the outline for a design onto the surface of the pot.

The next stage of the design is now considered. A first drawing is done on the pot in a thin, light-grey tone of Chinese ink. Since this is a carbon-based ink all traces of this marking-out will burn away during the enamel firing. Russell finds it important to spend some time getting this first draft accurate, as mistakes will take more time to rectify later on. The actual outline is painted over the Chinese ink draft and is a solution of manganese dioxide mixed with the liquid strained from an infusion of green tea, and mulled on a glass slab to a very fine powder. The dark, almost black manganese pigment shows up in a sharp contrast to the faint grey line of Chinese ink, which is very convenient since where the design has been outlined and where it needs to be overpainted can be seen clearly.

Another method Russell employs for sketching out his designs is to produce his own transfers; this is particularly useful when applying the central design to a plate, and can save a lot of time. First the design is traced from the sketchbook in ballpoint pen onto a good quality tissue paper; on the reverse of this tracing the outline is overpainted using very finely ground charcoal mixed with water — the finer ground the charcoal is the more prints can be pulled from each transfer. These tracings can then be directly applied to the gelatine coated pots by gently rubbing over the ballpoint side of the tracing, so the fine charcoal is deposited on the surface of the pot. Sometimes, however, the manganese outline is painted directly onto the pot without the guidelines given by the Chinese ink outlines or the charcoal transfers.

After the design outline has been made and the pot has been allowed to dry for a day, the work is ready to receive the enamels. The enamels are manufactured by means of a precise and thorough technique. At present Russell uses five basic colours, yellow, red, purple, green and blue. Each enamel is a semi-transparent glass, except for the red whose finished appearance is more matt, thin and opaque. Each of the coloured glasses are formulated as separate recipes using the triaxial blending method, which enables Russell to create precisely balanced enamels which will mature, melt and 'fall' at the same time. This is very important; if the same base glaze is used for each colour then the

8 Left: Decoration on the glazed pot begins with the outlining of a design in Chinese ink (which burns away in the firing).

9 Right: The Chinese ink is overpainted using manganese ground to a fine pigment with green tea liquer.

10 The glazed pot with its underglaze blue and manganese outline is now ready to receive the enamels.

Four triaxial blends for purple, yellow, blue and green enamel colours are shown here, together with a line blend for red enamel glaze, containing from 5 to 40% red iron oxide.

various colouring oxides which are added will act as secondary fluxes, and the enamels will begin to melt at different temperatures. The worst possible combination here would be the green melting first, the yellow remaining immature and cloudy and the purple boiling and bubbling. It is therefore crucial that Russell knows exactly how his materials will react and which formulas will be compatible in the melting temperatures. Although this precision is necessary for a physically compatible palette, the density of colour is purely a matter of personal taste: Russell knows through experience the percentage of oxides that will give him the colour he wants. The actual colour density may be arrived at by his having established a line blend of the oxide and the base glaze. Red, for instance, may contain anything up to 40% of red iron oxide, giving a wide range of subtle colour.

'The red which I use is a deep Kutani red. It is painted on quite thinly and can also be used as a wash. In old Kutani ware red was used sparingly, the design being composed largely of four brilliant glassy colours, yellow, green, blue and purple.

In Imari ware the red is sometimes applied more thickly and is used in conjunction with underglaze blue and gold. The Kakiemon red, which is of great renown, is more orange, and forms a large part of the designs with a soft green and distinctive azure blue on a milky-white porcelain body. All of these Japanese reds beautifully complement the other enamel colours with which they are used. In their making the most important ingredient would seem to be red iron oxide, which is extremely finely ground.'

After many thorough tests the correct recipe for each enamel is arrived at and the pigment is ground to a fine powder. The grinding is done firstly in a pestle and mortar (50 grams at a time) and then mixed with water and a syrupy solution of boiled seaweed (bought as a dried plant which is boiled in water and strained through a cotton cloth). The mixture and pigment is then further ground on a glass tile with a porcelain muller. To make a good colour (particularly the red) the medium has to be ground for approximately twenty minutes for each 10 gram of enamel, and each colour has a set of preparation and application equipment (glass tiles, mullers and brushes), so there is little danger of colours crossing.

11 Boiled seaweed liquer is used to form a thick viscous liquid when ground with the enamel.

12 Below left: Enamels are thickly applied over the pot because they will form a transparent glass. The manganese line underneath will show through.

13 Below right: The pot awaiting enamel firing.

The enamels are applied with a brush when they are the consistency of double cream. The colour is allowed to drip from the brush end, and spread within the boundaries of the manganese outline. This 'floating' method of application ensures that the manganese outline is not disturbed and that the enamel forms a thick enough layer, $\frac{1}{2}$ mm to $1\frac{1}{2}$ mm in depth.

The thickness of the enamel is critical to the overall finished quality of the work, different thicknesses giving differing densities of colour. Skilful application is required to create a uniformly coloured large flat area – however, differences in colour density can be, and are, used as a decorative device. Russell avoids touching the surface of the pot with his fingers during the painting, since finger grease can cause unsightly black specks and any unavoidable contact, such as placing the pot in the kiln, is on undecorated areas which can be cleaned with the gelatine solution.

Then the pots are placed in a small electric kiln (6.5 cu ft) and fired to around the 840°C mark; plates are fired on their edges. The correct melt of the enamels is monitored by the use of draw trials – small tiles painted with each of the enamels are suspended in the kiln on copper wire. They are drawn from the kiln at regular intervals (near to the maturing temperature) and are inspected after cooling in water.

This way Russell can monitor the 'fall' of the melting enamels, that is, the slight flow and movement of the slowly melting coloured glazes, and it enables him to shut down the kiln when all the colours have reached the optimum point of maturity, freezing the enamels in a wet, jewel-like moment of fluidity.

Combining the knowledge he gained of this specialised area of ceramics in Japan with his own particular awareness and his training as a painter, Russell Coates has established a form of decoration both innovative in design and highly skilled in its technology. While retaining the traditional qualities of Japanese enamelling his work reflects the diversity of an ever-enquiring mind and an ever-seeking eye.

Photography by John Coles.

Opposite: Enamelled porcelain vase, 8½ inches high, 7½ inch diameter.

Enamelled porcelain decorated plate, 15 inch diameter.

Technical information

Porcelain glaze
85% cornish stone
15% whiting

Underglaze blue
30% cobalt blue
16% manganese dioxide
 4% nickel oxide
50% kaolin

Violet enamel
80% lead bisilicate
20% lead borax frit
 1% manganese dioxide

Green enamel
75.5% lead bisilicate
 4.5% quartz
20% lead borax frit
 5% copper oxide

Red enamel
76% lead bisilicate
 4% quartz
20% lead borax frit
30% red iron oxide

Yellow enamel
49.2% lead bisilicate
 4.8% quartz
46% lead borax frit
 4% red iron oxide

Blue enamel
78.5% lead bisilicate
 1.5% quartz
20% lead borax frit
 0.8% cobalt oxide

John Wheeldon

'I went to art college because it seemed to me at the time to be a natural progression from doing art at school. I began by studying graphics, but soon gravitated towards the ceramics department because the lecturers were much friendlier and the atmosphere was comfortable and easy to work in.'

After leaving college, nearly all of the work John Wheeldon produced was functional. His first pottery was in Sudbury Hall in Derbyshire, and here he made a range of simple, direct domestic ware using one or two basic standard glazes. During his last firing at Sudbury John first delved into the realms of decoration, and began to formulate many of the ideas which now affect his work. Through experiments with various decorative techniques, such as using a slip trailer filled with glaze, stamping and impressing clay, a quite definite method and philosophy began to emerge.

John has always been interested in the skills used in precision engineering, and this fascination with the detailed structure of manufactured machine parts was one of the many influences which contributed to the development of his recent work. After moving to a new house and pottery in an old public house in Derbyshire, John needed to find a way of expressing some of the ideas he'd previously only touched upon during his forays into decorative effects.

Searching for a clay which would act as a vehicle for these new ideas led John to develop a black basalt body from a recipe given to him by another potter. The basic constituents were a very plastic ball clay, china clay and molochite (calcined china clay which acts as a grog or opener to give the clay a coarse texture and increase its refractory qualities). Various metal oxides are added in heavy quantities to this clay, which when fired in a neutral atmosphere to stoneware temperatures creates a dense black-coloured clay. As a contrast with this clay, John also began to produce white pots based upon a porcelain clay.

The three main forms John makes and decorates are bowls, boxes and vases — his vase form is based on a Neolithic grain storage jar he once saw in a Nottingham museum. Yet when choosing the shapes to make with the new black clay, John had a natural preference for the bowl; the bowl, for him, acted as a picture with the rim as a frame and the centrally curved, glazed area as the stretched canvas. The curve of the bowl contributes to the feeling of tension contained by the black, unglazed frame of the rim, and at the making stage the curve is considered with regard to the later lustre decoration. The angle at which the bowl lifts from the footring can determine what kind of vessel it is to become — a steep-sided bowl will give a feeling of enclosing space, a flatter curve will be more open and 'giving'. These are important considerations as to how the piece will be decorated, and in any case John is very interested in arches and curves; he is aware of the spring and elegance in a curve as he throws his bowls.

Bowl, c. 6 inch diameter, precious lustres on a cone 8 glaze.

Rims are equally important in the finished work; a rolled, soft rim gives a warm homely effect, whilst a torn, flat rim, with the grog literally pulled out by the action of the throwing rib and the momentum of the wheel) produces a harsh, staccato border finish, where the central glazed area is heavily accentuated by the dramatic black intensity of the unglazed rim.

When throwing his pots on the kickwheel, John starts to make decisions on where the areas of glaze will be and where the enamel and lustres will be placed. After drying and biscuit firing the pieces are waxed with a mixture of candlewax and white spirit in order to resist the glaze; this determines which areas of the black clay pots are glazed or remain unglazed. John's porcelain pieces are nearly always glazed all over.

Initially the black body John created threw well and fired satisfactorily, but he was disappointed by the dead qualities of the finished glaze. Whatever glaze he used would be saturated by the heavy overloading of the metal oxides in the clay body. This saturation would produce a dark green glaze which had a good fit and smooth surface, but had no brightness in colour, or visual depth.

'It was during this period that I saw a small exhibition; just a few cases of Hispano-Moresque pottery, covered in beautiful lustres – but it was enough to spark off many of the ideas I had been harbouring with relation to the black basalt pots.'

The exhibition that John saw led him to the bright realms of lustre decoration. The bright rich colours of gold and precious metal lustres were ideal for use upon the flat green glazes, contrasting vibrantly with the dense black clay. And the very nature of the boxes John makes is appropriate for gold and precious metal lustre decoration:

'I feel that small lidded boxes should contain something intimate and precious, so I decorate them with this feeling in mind – and the top of a lid is a great surface to decorate, too.'

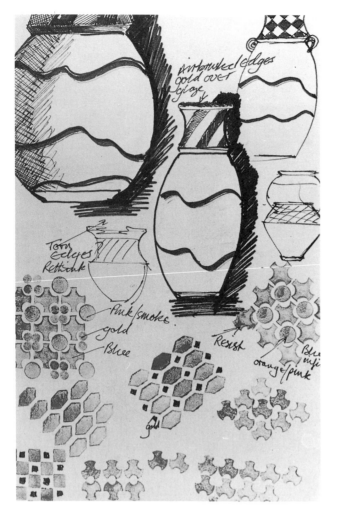

John's interest in geometry and ordered structures is evident in his method of applying lustres and in the motifs involved. Using a particularly dense yet pliable foam rubber, whose thickness need only be $\frac{1}{4}$ inch, he punches out what will become the tips of his stamps. He uses sharpened metal punches made from various diameter pipes which can be squeezed and pinched to alter their original shape. With these punches John can stamp out either a blank shape, such as a square, circle, etc. or by cutting at the edges of a blank he can produce more intricate shapes such as stars, crosses, crescents and so on. A backing of thin cork is added to the foam rubber tip to increase its resilience and overall support, and then a handle of suitable size and thickness is added: John prefers to use old paint brush handles. When covered with a thin film of lustres the stamp moulds itself to the contours of the pot's surface, yet the support from the cork backing means that the image is clear, even and lies flat on the curving expanse of the bright shiny glaze.

After deciding on the images to be used on each pot, John begins the process of dividing and constructing patterns; his previous decisions on which areas to leave glazed or unglazed afford him a framework to work in. Masking tape can be used to give a sharply defined line on the glazed surface. If a tighter curve is required then designer's gouache is painted on the glazed surface – this resists the adhesion of the lustres to the glazed surface during firing and can be scrubbed off after the pots have been fired.

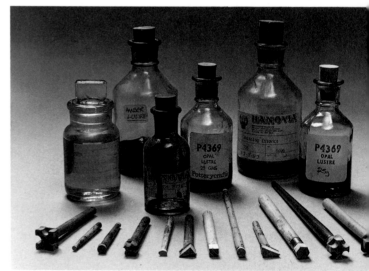

Page from John Wheeldon's sketchbook.

Right: Lustres and stamps used in his production.

1 Left: Cutting a stamp from rubber.

'The shape of the pot's surface decides for itself where the lines of pattern and demarcation will be. As Hamada once said "I ask the pot and it tells me how to decorate it."

After he has decided how the surface will be divided, John begins the process of decorating. Using his larger stamps, then infilling those areas with smaller stamps creates complex, rhythmic movements of shape and colour, each sub-divided area being counterbalanced in scale and resonance and giving an overall effect of rich visual texture. The quality of patterning created in this process can almost be likened to that of woven textiles, such as carpets, tapestries, printed fabrics and other forms of weaving, and John finds weaving is a major influence.

'I tend to see patterns everywhere, from the Norman stone carvings in the church next door to the advertising material in the pub down the road.'

Colours play an important role in the final qualities John achieves, and his choice of colour falls broadly into two

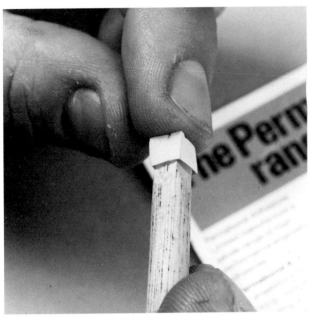

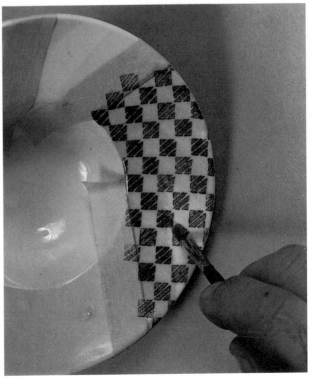

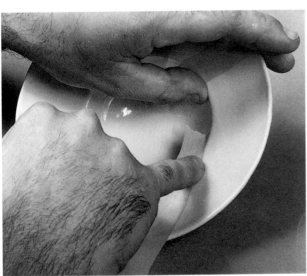

2 Above left: Attaching the stamp to a handle.

3 Below left: Masking out areas of the pot.

4 Above right: Stamping on poster paint which resists the lustre and prevents the lustre from adhering to the pot during firing.

5 Below right: Painting the lustre over the poster paint resist.

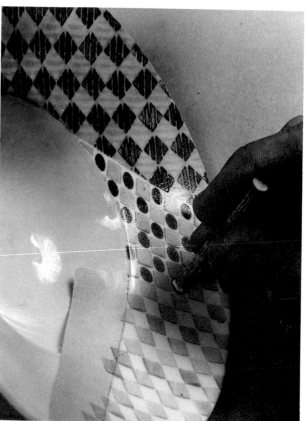

Above left: Detail of surface decoration.

6 Below left: Stamping the lustre onto lustre in between the resist pattern.

7 Above right: Building up the pattern.

8 Below right: Painting on the lustre in the centre of the pot, spinning it on a banding wheel to create a swirling brush pattern.

camps, dictated to some extent by the very nature of the two clays he uses, the black clay and the white porcelain. All of the subtly coloured lustres, such as yellow, pale blue and so on, will disappear or be overwhelmed if used on the heavily stained black body, saturating through the glaze. For this reason he relies on the strong metals, copper, bronze and gold for decorating the black pots. The porcelain pieces which are glazed all over offer much more scope for a wide range of subtle colour combinations. Very often the porcelain pots are enclosed bowls, which are heavily decorated on the rims and act as a frame for the enveloped inner space of the deeply curved bowl.

The inner curves of the porcelain bowls are brushed in a swirling motion using soft jewel-like lustres, such as mother of pearl or other light lustres – this introduces an element of mysterious movement to the centre of the pot,

while the heavily decorated rim contains and frames this quality. These pieces are a vivid contrast to the dramatic black-rimmed, black-bodied open forms of the copper, bronze and gold decorated pieces.

The lustre firing is carried out in an antiquated top-loading kiln with an ill-fitting lid (ideal for plenty of ventilation). Cone 018 is used for determining the temperature at which the lustres mature. The golds, bronzes and copper are fired in the cooler areas at the bottom of the kiln, as John finds that these lustres have a better quality colour if fired in a cooler place. The kiln is only 6 cu ft in size, which means that a quick turnaround in both ideas and production can be achieved.

Four porcelain bowls, c. 6 inch diameters, coloured lustres on a white base glaze.

Technical information

Black clay

55% HVAR ball clay
15% china clay
30% molochite (30s to dust mesh)

added to this basic clay are the following oxides:

3.3% manganese
3.3% iron
1.6% copper
1.6% cobalt

Because there is a high level of the non-plastic material molochite in this recipe, it is recommended to use the most plastic ball clay which can be afforded. Similarly a high plastic china clay greatly improves the clay's workability. Molochite (calcined china clay) adds texture and refractory qualities to the clay, enabling relatively high temperatures to be achieved before the added oxides act as a flux and cause the clay to slag and slump.

Porcelain

The porcelain is a standard clay produced by Valentine's.

Glaze recipes

Matte eggshell pink

62.5% feldspar
18.5% dolomite
18.5% china clay

Cone 8 glaze *(Bernard Leach)*

40% feldspar
30% flint
20% whiting
10% china clay

An addition of 5% talc is included in this recipe.

Both these glazes are used upon the black clay body and the porcelain.

Zircon glaze

38% potash feldspar
 7% whiting
11.5% talc
17.5% china clay
26% flint
 8% zircon

This glaze is used primarily on the inside area of the porcelain bowls, giving a bright, shiny, craze-resistant finish.

Lustres

The following lustres are used on the porcelain pieces:
opal, orange, pink, turquoise, copper, red, brown, light blue, mother of pearl, black yellow, smoke. All are commercial lustres purchased from Englehards Hanovia Sales, Gloucestershire, except smoke, which is a Johnson Mattey product.

The following lustres are used on the black pieces:
gold, copper, bronze, purple (black lustre gives purple results when used upon the black clay pots).

Occasionally slips of 50% ball clay, 50% china clay with the addition of commercial body stains are sprayed lightly across the surface of the porcelain pots before biscuit firing, which very slightly shades the otherwise flat white surface.

Photography by John Coles.

Detail of surface decoration.

Gallery

Alan Peascod (Australia)
'Form', 15¾ inches high. Copper and
silver lustre. The reduced lustre pigment
is wood fired with white pine to a
working temperature of 650–700°C.
Decoration is by sgraffito and brush.

Geoffrey Swindell (UK)
Three porcelain wheelmade lidded pots,
c. 4 inches high. Fired to Orton cone 9
with copper oxide in dolomite and
titanium type glazes, and onglaze lustre
resist technique.

David Taylor (UK)
Oval serving dish, 13 × 11 × 8 inches. Overglaze enamels on white glazed earthenware.

Patrick Loughran (USA)
Kidney dinnerware, dinner plate 12 × 8 inches. Glazed earthenware with lustres.

Paul Mathieu (Canada)
'Incarnation' 13¾ × 13¾ × 6 inches. Press moulded porcelain (6 pieces). Rim altered, 2 plates, 2 bowls, 1 cup and saucer. High fire glazes with overglazes and lustres.

Gallery

Jamie McCrae (Canada)
Above left: 'Memory jar', 10 inches high, seashells with fish scales, green underglaze pencil, clear glaze, gold lustre.

Mary Rich (UK)
Below right: Bottle, porcelain, $5\frac{1}{2} \times 19$ inches high. Purple glaze, copper and gold lustre.

Judy Trim (UK)
Below left: 'Tear Jar', 9 inches high, 1986. Red clay burnished, with metal lustres.

List of suppliers

The following list gives only those suppliers mentioned by the potters featured in this book. For a more comprehensive list of suppliers readers are referred to *The Potter's Dictionary of Materials and Techniques* by Frank and Janet Hamer (second edition 1986, published by A & C Black).

UK

Potclays Ltd
Brickkiln Lane
Etruria
Stoke on Trent ST4 7BP
Tel. 0782–29816

(general supplies and prepared clays)

Potterycrafts Ltd
Campbell Road
Stoke on Trent ST4 4ET
Tel. 0782–272 444

(general supplies)

Ferro (Great Britain) Ltd
Wombourne
Wolverhampton WV5 8DA
Tel. 0902–894 144

(general supplies)

Moira Pottery Co Ltd
Burton on Trent DE12 6DF
Tel. 0283–221 961

(prepared clays)

Watts Blake Bearne & Co Ltd
Park House
Courtenay Park
Newton Abbot
Devon TQ12 4PS
Tel. 0626–2345

(powdered clay)

English China Clays Ltd
John Keay House
St Austell
Cornwall PL25 4DJ
Tel. 0726–4482
(Distributed by Whitfield & Son Ltd,
23 Albert St, Newcastle, Staffs)

(powdered clays)

Varcoes Sales Co Ltd
St Austell
Cornwall

(molochite)

Morgan Refractories Ltd
Liverpool Rd
Weston
Wirral
Cheshire
Tel. 051–336 3911

('T' material)

Blythe Colours Ltd
Creswell
Stoke on Trent
Tel. 0782–395 959

(ceramic colours)

Medcol
Sun Street
Hanley
Stoke on Trent
Staffs

(colours)

USA

Ferro Corporation
PO Box 6650
Cleveland
Ohio 44101

(general supplies)

Pemco Products Group
5601 Eastern Avenue
Baltimore
Maryland 21224

(frits and general)

Cedar Heights Clay Company
50 Portsmouth Rd
Oak Hill
Ohio

(clays)

Mason Colour & Chemical
PO Box 76
East Liverpool
Ohio 43920

(colours)

Orton pyrometric cones
(The Edward Orton Jr Ceramic Foundation, Westerville, Ohio)

Large cones; squatting temperatures when heated at:

Cone no.	60°C/hr	108°F/hr	150°C/hr	270°F/hr
022	576*	1069*	586*	1086*
021	602	1116	614	1137
020	625	1157	635	1175
019	668	1234	683	1261
018	696	1285	717	1323
017	727	1341	747	1377
016	764	1407	792	1458
015	790	1454	804	1479
014	834	1533	838	1540
013	836*	1537*	861*	1582*
012	856*	1573*	872*	1602*
011	872*	1602*	883*	1621*
010	880*	1616*	890*	1634*
09	915	1679	923	1693
08	945	1733	955	1751
07	973	1783	984	1803
06	991	1816	999	1830
05	1031	1888	1046	1915

Large cones; squatting temperatures when heated at:

Cone no.	60°C/hr	108°F/hr	150°C/hr	270°F/hr
04	1050	1922	1060	1940
03	1086	1987	1101	2014
02	1101	2014	1120	2048
01	1117	2043	1137	2079
1	1136	2077	1154	2109
2	1142	2088	1162	2124
3	1152	2106	1168	2134
4	1168	2134	1186	2167
5	1177	2151	1196	2185
6	1201	2194	1222	2232
7	1215	2219	1240	2264
8	1236	2257	1263	2305
9	1260	2300	1280	2336
10	1285	2345	1305	2381
11	1294	2361	1315	2399
12	1306	2383	1326	2419
13	1321	2410	1346	2455
14	1388	2530	1366	2491

1 The temperature equivalents shown for the large cones may be used as a guideline for determining deformation temperatures of self-supporting cones. However the self-supporting cones may deform at approximately 2°C higher than the large cones depending on the mounting height of the large cones.

2 *These temperatures are approximate. They were not determined at the National Bureau of Standards.

Reproduced from *The Potter's Dictionary of Materials and Techniques*, second edition, by Frank and Janet Hamer (A & C Black, 1986).

Index

Index